AN ENQUIRY INTO THE POLICY OF MAKING CONQUESTS

AN ENQUIRY INTO THE POLICY OF MAKING CONQUESTS

FOR THE

MAHOMETANS IN INDIA

William Burke

GYAN

Published by

Gyan Publishing House
5, Ansari Road
Daryaganj, New Delhi-110002
Phone: 011-47034999, 9811692060
E-mail: books@gyanbooks.com

Distribution Network
gyanbooks.com
India, USA, Canada, UK, Australia, France

ISBN : 978-81-212-9646-5 (PB)
First Published, 1779

2nd Impression 2023

Printed at: Gyan Press, Delhi.

AN ENQUIRY INTO THE POLICY OF MAKING CONQUESTS
Author: WILLIAM BURKE

AN ENQUIRY INTO THE POLICY OF MAKING CONQUESTS FOR THE MAHOMETANS in INDIA, BY THE *BRITISH* ARMS;

In ANSWER, to a PAMPHLET, INTITULED

"CONSIDERATIONS "ON THE "CONQUEST OF TANJORE."

AN

ENQUIRY

INTO THE

POLICY, &c.

SECTION I.

Character and merits of the Nabob prove nothing in favour of his conquest of Tanjore.—Can have no right to possess himself of that country on account of the matters with which he charges the King of Tanjore.—Nature of those charges.

THE success of the British arms in Hindostan, during the last war, has brought us into very close connexions with many of the Princes of that country, both Indian and Mahometan. Their several rights wholly depending upon the British power, must be finally determined upon by the British justice. Among the innumerable controversies concerning Indian claims, those of the King of Tanjore, and Mahomet Ali Khawn, Nabob of Arcot, have lately attracted the greatest share of the public attention.

The

The contraſt between the proceedings of theſe two powers, which is very ſtrongly marked in every reſpect, has been in no inſtance more ſtriking than in the manner of their ſeeking redreſs for the injuries they reſpectively complain of.

From the year 1769, if not from a more early period, the Nabob has engaged a number of perſons to act for him in Europe, in a great variety of ways. Theſe gentlemen have endeavoured to recommend themſelves to their employer by their extraordinary zeal and activity in his ſervice; and their pretenſions to that kind of merit are not wholly without foundation. They have been indefatigable in their intrigues and publications. They have filled the world with many new topics of argument, and new narratives of fact. They have even been at the pains of correcting and amending hiſtory; in order to accommodate it to his views, and for the ſake of ſetting us right, not only with regard to his character and pretenſions, but even to his pedigree. Nothing on their ſide has been wanting to form a party in his favour. He had great objects in view, which were not to be compaſſed but by the arms of the Engliſh. It was therefore natural, that nothing ſhould be omitted which might tend to obtain the authority, or at leaſt the connivance, of Great Britain, in the uſe, which he had already made, and which he was ſtill in hopes of making, of the power of this kingdom in India.

The King of Tanjore, on the other hand, having had no ſuch views of conqueſt, having nothing to expect from our force, and having for a long time no apprehenſions from our violence,

violence *, was satisfied to preserve his intercourse with this country, solely through the ordinary channels of office.

Three solemn treaties violated—two invasions—two plunderings of his country—two years imprisonment of his person—made no alteration in his plan. He expected justice, in the ordinary course of business, from the authority that the nation has made competent to give it. He has in some measure found it; and it is to be hoped, that at length he will find it more perfectly.

Not one person, during this long period of his sufferings, has ever once endeavoured, on his part, to interest the public in his favour. If we have at all been apprised of the injuries he has sustained from his powerful neighbour, the Nabob of Arcot, it has incidentally arisen from the sort of propriety that others have felt of vindicating their own character, and their public conduct, from the aspersions of the active and vindictive partisans of the Nabob.

It was this sense of honour that impelled the Directors of the East India Company, and the family of Lord Pigot, to make those appeals to the public, which have fully justified the national wisdom in its act of justice and sound policy, the restoration of the kingdom of Tanjore to its original and rightful owner.

This extraordinary reserve of the Tanjoreans, whether oweing to moderation or remissness, has given the enemies of that

* See the assurances of English protection pledged to him. Company's Papers, Appendix, No. 8.

unhappy people great advantages over them. Beſides the operation of direct agency againſt them, the very channels of communication between India and Europe have been vitiated by being ſecured by a party. Redreſs from a remote protector is always tardy, and generally incomplete. It is a part of the reparation of old injuries to provide ſome ſecurity againſt new ones. For the fictions and fallacies which have produced former miſchiefs, when their ill foundation is forgotten, in the firſt act of redreſs, are, by the unceaſing activity of ambition, frequently revived. This has been very lately the caſe, in the attempts to renew the exploded topics for eſtabliſhing a ſyſtem of conqueſt by Engliſh arms, in favour of the Nabob of Arcot; the conſtant purſuit of which, for twenty years, has brought innumerable and unſpeakable calamities on all the ſouthern part of Hindoſtan, and reduced ſo many conſiderable Princes, ſuch numbers of reſpectable Nobility, and the induſtrious inhabitants of ſo many once flouriſhing and opulent countries, to the laſt degree of indigence and diſtreſs, to ſay nothing of the multitude of lives which have been loſt in theſe extravagant enterprizes, which had their riſe in this fatal deſign.

The humanity, the juſtice and the honour of the nation, are intereſted in the uſe which is made of the formidable power it has acquired in the Eaſt; and we ought to look carefully into thoſe pretended rights of Princes and Conquerors, recommended to us in ſuch a multiplicity of writings, whenever they are to be exerciſed by the

7 ſubverſion

ſubverſion of ancient and reſpectable eſtabliſhments. A conqueror, who ſupports his own pride by his own power, may be very unjuſt, but he is not ridiculous—but nothing is ſo contemptible in the eye of reaſon as extreme ambition, depending upon extrinſic force; and which is a ſuppliant, not for protection, but for ſuperiority, dominion, and conqueſt. The purpoſe of all the manœuvres, and all the publications, on the part of the Nabob, is to prevail on us to make him a great conqueror by our violence.

An addition has lately been made to theſe publications, by a Pamphlet, called "Conſiderations on the Conqueſt of "Tanjore." It did not ſeem very neceſſary to revive the diſcuſſion of a queſtion, which after many violent diſputes, and many great ſtruggles, has been ſettled by a competent authority. By that ſettlement, the King of Tanjore was re-eſtabliſhed on the throne of his anceſtors, under the protection of the Eaſt India Company, and in a condition of intire dependence upon Great Britain *.

An eſtabliſhment for any country which is ſettled under the dominion of its natural ſovereign, a ſovereign connected with his ſubjects in affections, manners, and religion, and at the ſame time ſecured in a ſtate of abſolute ſubſerviency to the intereſt of this kingdom, ſeems to be too ſolidly built, upon foundations both of juſtice and of good policy, to make an undertaking to overturn it, a very plauſible project.

The profeſſed purpoſe of the Pamphlet before us (of which

* The terms by which he was re-eſtabliſhed, are before the Reader in an Appendix.

its

its author ſays a great many good things) is nothing leſs than a modeſt propoſal for the King and Parliament to abdicate their authority over Tanjore; and to ſurrender the ſovereign of that nation, and his people, into the hands of a Mahometan deſpot, the bitter and implacable enemy of that ſovereign and that people. It propoſes that this ſhould be adopted by, or forced upon, the Eaſt India Company; which is to be made the inſtrument of a *third* revolution, in direct violation of its own faith, moſt ſolemnly and recently given; in violation of terms preſcribed by the Company itſelf, and punctually complied with, in every particular, by the King of Tanjore.

In an attempt againſt poſſeſſion *ſo* ſupported, in favour of a Pretender on the moſt odious of all claims, *a ſuppoſed right of conqueſt*, the author ought to have done ſomething more than repeat the arguments which have been ſo often refuted. It is, I admit, no objection againſt an argument, that it has been uſed before; but then, in a renewed controverſy, the adverſe party is obliged to take the matter in its new ſtate. He is bound to conſider the original argument and its anſwer together, and, by ſhewing the futility of the latter, to confirm, if he can, the former in its firſt authority. Without ſome obſervation of this rule, controverſies can have no end.

The author of theſe "Conſiderations" ſets out with more profeſſions of candour and decorum than, I think, I have ever met with in any political publication. But I muſt beg leave to ſay, that he ſupports theſe profeſſions very indifferently, and that he is neither very decent to his adverſaries,

nor

nor very refpectful to his reader, in not attempting to reply to the anfwers that have been fo often made to the arguments he ufes. He is not to be fuffered to evade the performance of this indifpenfible duty, by telling us in a high tone "* *WE* have carefully avoided the difgufting paths "of controverfy, the affertions equally confident and unfounded, the quotations equally partial and inconclufive, "in fhort, the complicated arrogance and fallacy, in which "fome writers on this fubject have indulged themfelves."

That in "fome late publications, the writers jumbling "together perfons and things, and mixing calumny with fo-"phiftry, are generally poffeffed of a convenient inattention "to the facts and arguments of their opponents."

That "their arguments are fupported by felf-references; "and their facts are proved by garbled appendixes."

This profeffion of avoiding the paths of controverfy, in a *controverted* matter, is rather new; and as to the character this author gives to fome other performances, how far it is applicable to his own mode of writing, rather than to that of his adverfaries, will be feen hereafter. But, fince he does not choofe to quote thofe whom he choofes in this manner to afperfe, it is neceffary the Reader fhould know who the writers are whom he treats with a contempt, which, however politic, is not very agreeable to the modefty and moderation he profeffes. The firft of thefe writers is Mr. Rous, a member of Parliament, and a barrifter of acknowledged

* Confiderations, pages 29 and 30.

abilities

abilities and learning; the accuracy and judgment of whofe performance † has fully juftified the opinion the world had conceived of his talents. This gentleman, had he not been entitled to better treatment on account of his own acknowledged merits, had ftill a claim to fome fort of attention from the authority under which he writes. His work is undertaken with the fanction, and by the exprefs defire of the Directors of the Eaft India Company. He is fupplied with his materials out of their records, and he produces them in order to refute the rafh charges againft that refpectable body, contained in two Pamphlets, one intituled, "*State of Facts relative to Tanjore*;" and the other intituled, "*Original Papers relative to Tanjore*." Thofe pamphlets are, in reality, the foundation of the work now before us.—The other gentleman he alludes to does not put his name to his book; but he too is known to be a barrifter, and a man of confiderable parts, and eminent in the literary world.

Without recriminating on the author of the "Confiderations;" without enquiring into his own inducements, views, and defigns, or without accufing him of deception or fophiftry, or of complicated arrogance and fallacy, or charging him with any party or interefted motive, I will content myfelf with examining into his reafons for the *new revolution he propofes to effect, by delivering the kingdom of Tanjore into the hands of the Nabob of Arcot*.

† "The Reftoration of the King of Tanjore confidered;" printed by order of the Directors of the Eaft India Company, in 1777.

His

His work begins, and ends, and is interlarded throughout, with a panegyric on that great Muſſulman Lord. An anſwer to this part of his work will not add greatly to the bulk of mine. In expatiating on the virtues and merits of his Highneſs, Mahomed Ali Khawn, he ſhall have no ſort of interruption from me. He has the field all to himſelf. I am the more willing to indulge him in his free career; becauſe the fulleſt admiſſion of all the virtues and merits that truth or flattery can heap on the Nabob, will not give the leaſt aſſiſtance to his cauſe: It will not prove, that he has the leaſt particle of right to depoſe the King of Tanjore; or that it is either the duty or the intereſt of the Engliſh nation to put that kingdom under a Mahometan yoke.

What the author ſays of the alliance of this Mahometan potentate, with Great Britain—the nature of that alliance—the terms of it—and the benefit we have derived from the connexion, are all as little worth confuting. The author admits, that the Nabob, on his part, has derived reciprocal advantages from his connexion with Great Britain. — In truth, he has derived every thing from it, fortune, dominion, life itſelf. Flying from a battle, where his father had loſt his life, and his *elder Brother* was made priſoner, in the ruin of his fortunes, and in preference to that *elder Brother*, (who is ſtill alive) the Engliſh arms ſhielded him both againſt his foreign enemies, and the ſtrong domeſtic pretenſion of his own family. Whatever Great Britain is ſaid by his advocate to have received from his bounty, (and

C of

of which he has made out an extraordinary bill *) is in fact but a very small portion, which she has reserved to herself from conquests that were made, (we may fairly say) altogether by her own arms: all the rest is her gift to him. But whether the balance in this matter be on his side, or on ours, signifies very little; the point in question is only this, "Whether our alliance with him be so exclusive as to render "all other alliances impossible or improper;" or, in particular, "that we were ever bound by the terms of our alliance to "conquer for him the kingdom of Tanjore;—or are now "bound to depose that King, whom, by a solemn public act "we have just re-established?"

Until his friends shew such a condition, in the terms of our treaty with him, the Nabob's being the best, or the King of Tanjore the worst ally in the world, are matters worthy neither of proof nor refutation. If the author's invectives against the unhappy Prince, so cruelly plundered by his friend and patron, were admitted to have a foundation in fact, which they by no means have, it might prove that he ought to be punished, or restrained, or, (if he will) even deposed; but they would not prove that the Nabob of Arcot ought to be put into possession of a country which does not belong to him.

In the first place, it is proper to observe, that if the King of Tanjore, the present possessor, has not behaved as he

* Consid. pages 3, 4, 5.

ought to have done, (which is not admitted, and never can be proved) his misbehaviour does not forfeit the just claim of his family, or his tribe, to a kingdom which has always gone in succession. Much less does it forfeit the right of the native inhabitants, to be governed by Princes of their own religion and manners. This has been virtually admitted even by Mahomet Ali himself; for, whilst his ambition was young and modest, he pretended nothing further than a desire of placing another Prince of the same blood upon the throne of that kingdom.

2dly, It is to be remembered, that if the King of Tanjore has misbehaved, so as to incur a forfeiture, it is not the Nabob, but their common superior, the Grand Mogul, who has in that case the right to hear the cause, to adjudge the offence, to pronounce the sentence, and to allot the disposition of the forfeiture.

3dly, The reader is called upon to remark, that no evidence is before the Company or the Nation, of the truth of any one material charge made against the King of Tanjore.—The Nabob's advocate has not produced, nor even attempted to produce, any sort of *proofs* of any delinquency at any time. His method is, first to advance the Nabob's own charges as facts; and then, (as it is usual in such cases) he supplies the total defect of evidence, by the utmost profusion of railing and abuse.

It would be matter of eternal infamy to those who possess the smallest attention to justice, to receive the mere as-

 sertions

ſertions of a man deeply intereſted in the queſtion, either as proofs of a right on his own part, or of a puniſhable delinquency on that of the party whom he attacks; eſpecially when it is for the purpoſe of inducing a lucrative forfeiture in his own favour. Inſtead of expecting to be called on for rigid proofs in ſupport of ſuch harſh claims, the party of Mahomet Ali think they have done full enough, in juſtification of revolutions, wars, and devaſtations, when they give us a ſtring of ſurmiſes, ſuſpicions, and invectives, as if they were unqueſtionable and acknowledged truths perfectly known to the whole world. " What miſchiefs," ſays this author *, " may be apprehended from reſtoring a coun-" try ſo ſituated, ſo circumſtanced, to the ſway of a man " ſo notoriouſly abandoned to all ties of duty, faith, and " honour, as the Rajah of Tanjore? Are the dark ſchemes " he formed with Monſieur Lally, to ſeize on Trichino-" poly, forgotten? Are his after-plottings with Hyder Alli, " Iſoph Cawn, and other powers, dangerous and inimical " to the Company, totally obliterated? Is he not at this " inſtant, though ſcarcely ſeated on the throne of his an-" ceſtors, engaged with Hyder in a deep intrigue with the " Chevalier St. Aubin, a daring and wily adventurer, ſent " out by Monſieur Sartine, the French miniſter?"

This ſort of ſpecimen of their mode of accuſation I have thought fit to lay before the reader. To explain at large all theſe matters here huddled together would require a

* Conſiderations, p. 52, and 53.

volume.

volume. But as the author has not thought fit to take any notice of the satisfactory answers already given to most of these calumnies, I think it sufficient to refer the reader to the books already mentioned; I mean the Company's publication, through Mr. Rous, and the Defence of Lord Pigot. With regard to the last insinuation, concerning the present King of Tanjore, as I suppose it relates to things done since the publication of those pieces, I have only to observe, that the unfairness of the author is not excusable even by the licence of an advocate. He gives no proof; he cites no authority; and he supplies the want of evidence, by the supposed notoriety of a transaction which never has been heard of; which never did exist.

I shall further beg leave to remark, that this very dangerous person, (who has put the gentleman into such a flutter, by his deep intrigues with the Chevalier St. Aubin and Monsieur Sartine) has not a soldier in the world; that his house is guarded, and his capital is garrisoned by a body of English troops, which may be reinforced to any number; and that the far greater part of his clear revenue is given for their payment.

As to the Nabob's grievances, I suppose no one ever attempted to injure another, without some sort of complaint of injury supposed to be done, or intended, to himself; and if the mere complaint of a party is sufficient justification for consequent violences, no Prince can want an excuse to seize upon the possessions of his neighbour.—I would ask

this

this gentleman, who urges us ſo vehemently, to employ the Engliſh power and arms for ſuch worthy purpoſes, why neither he nor his friends have thought proper to produce the letters, or the treaties, or any other vouchers whatever, of the King of Tanjore's being the aggreſſor, in any acts or deſigns to the Nabob's prejudice, or to that of the Company, whoſe intereſt they ſo inceſſantly affect to connect with *his* ambition?

Nothing is more eaſy than to ſweep away this whole maſs of calumny. But it is playing the game of Slander, and raiſing it to importance, to treat it with the ſolemnity which belongs to grave accuſation. When *vouchers* of theſe manœuvres, charged on the King of Tanjore, are produced, it will be time enough to examine into their nature. Until the accuſations are made to the King of Tanjore himſelf, and he is called upon to anſwer for them, in a place where he may refute them, all theſe looſe aſſertions, made at 9,000 miles diſtance from him, and of which, except in the ſtile of vexatious general reproaches, he hears nothing at home, they muſt be conſidered in no other light, than as the moſt indecent pretexts that ever were employed to colour the proceedings of rapacity and ambition.

SECTION II.

Nature of the records produced by the author, examined.—To what objects, and by what means, the Company's approbation has been obtained.—The Company imposed upon by the servants in India.

IF the evidence of the Nabob himself, in favour of his own usurpation, is of no force, of as little is that of those who were his accomplices in his designs, or his instigators to them. * His advocate makes a great parade of his *solid* facts, of his authentic papers, and of his unquestionable *records*; all which prove (as he asserts) the *necessity* of the original conquest, the *guilt* of the Rajah of Tanjore, and the *propriety* of reinstating him (the Nabob) in the possession of that kingdom, which had been just rescued from his usurpation. A record is a very serious thing, and the best of all evidence; But every written paper is not a record. When records are stated *as evidence in a question of right*, they ought to be, 1st, papers either written by the party against whom they are produced, or admitted by him, as valid and authentic—or, 2dly, they ought to be documents of facts from indifferent persons;—or, 3dly, evidence taken juridically. But, I believe the reader will be surprised to find, that three-fourths of the pretended records, with which this pamphlet is filled, are neither more nor less than the mere representations of those servants of the Company, who were

* Consid. p. 17, 30, &c.

the

the instruments of the Nabob in his usurpation of Tanjore, representations made to their masters, the Directors, with a view to justify their own conduct. These letters may be admitted as *pleadings in the cause*; and as pleadings, they are good as far as the force of their reasoning goes; but it is the first time, that such representations were ever taken as *matters of fact*, or admitted as indisputable evidence, or as any evidence at all, when the question itself is, " Whether the " act which these representations are made to cover, was " justifiable or not?"

Of this nature is the correspondence of the *Select Committee at Madrass*, which in the Pamphlet before us is constantly adduced as unexceptionable evidence for the gentlemen of that Committee in their own cause; pompously cited as an authentic record, and as regularly referred to, as if it were the sworn testimony of indifferent and impartial persons, upon a judicial examination into the merits of the proceeding.

Some things, however, very material, are to be observed in these pretended records, besides their incurable invalidity as evidence: First, it is to be observed, that if they were admitted as unexceptionable testimony, they do not at all come up to the purpose for which the author produces them—for though the letters of the Select Committee at Madrass are very free in their invectives against the King of Tanjore, and frequently enforce the necessity of *humbling, reducing, chastising, compelling him to do justice to the*

Nabob,

Nabob, &c. &c. &c. yet they no where presume to tell their masters, that they have had a *conquest of that country, for the Nabob, in view*, nor do they in any place, endeavour to recommend *that* measure.

Secondly, The Committee itself has taken away all the authority which can be supposed to belong even to their own partial allegations, so far as they tend to a justification of hostilities against the King of Tanjore: for they are forced by truth to profess explicitly, that they have acted in that affair *against their own judgment*, and they urge the compulsion and necessity they were under, as their apology. "This government," say they *, "as *guarantees*, " *ought* to have marched a force to *maintain peace*, between " the complaining parties, to have required deputies from " *both, to state the demands* of each respectively, and, upon a " *fair discussion*, to have decided between them, and to have " enforced the decision, whether in favour of the Nabob, or " in favour of the Rajah; but your government here did " *not dare* to act such a part. It was plain from your or- " ders to this Committee, under date the 17 March 1769, " as well as subsequent orders, that you thought the Rajah " stood in a degree of favour with this government, which " you did not approve; and that you adopted all the Na- " bob's ideas of levying crores, as an equitable pretension, be- " cause other Subahs had done so. At the same time the " minister of the crown, ranging himself on the side of the

* First volume of Company's Appendix, p. 180 and 181.

" Nabob, received all his complaints against the Rajah as
" gospel.

" Our conclusion is, that one of these decisive measures " should be adopted with firmness and vigour; either to take " Tanjore, openly and avowedly, under your protection, and " *give him proofs of your impartial justice*; which we think, *even* " *now, notwithstanding what has passed, will bind him firmly to* " *your interest*—or to conquer and subdue him totally :—but " in the latter case, the consequent arrangements will be " matter of the most serious consideration. What we said " on this subject by the Britannia contains our sense; and " since the year 1768, such lights have been thrown on *the* " *Nabob's character and conduct*, as may amply suffice to enable " your Honours to determine with justice and propriety; we " therefore only add, that every day convinces us we have " not been mistaken, and we confirm every word we have " wrote."

It is not material to the cause of Tanjore, to enquire whether the Select Committee at Madrass were or were not under the compulsion they alledge from the King's Commissioners in India, or from Administration here, or whether the Company thought them too partial to the King of Tanjore. We are not examining into the force of their apology for their conduct. It is plain, that *they were themselves of opinion against the part which they took*; that they were of opinion, that they ought to have *maintained peace*; that they ought to have *called on the parties* to make their respective demands; that they ought to have allowed *a fair discussion*, and *enforced an equitable decision*. They allow, that the King of Tanjore ought to have had *proofs of impartial justice*, which, they themselves declare, would bind him, *even now* (after all that has passed) to our interest: all this they allow to be their duty; they allow also that there is no part of this duty, that they have done. And this totally sets aside their authority, such as it is, for the rectitude of the measure they adopted; and rests the proof of that rectitude upon those whom they assert to have compelled them thus to act against their judgment.

As to the British Ministry, what authority for the Nabob's usurpation was given by them, I profess, I do not at all see. I do not find a syllable in the whole printed Correspondence, that tends to prove that they have authorized the *conquest* of Tanjore in favour of the Mahometans. If such orders had existed, I take it for granted, they would have been produced. The authority, therefore, supposed to be derived from the British Ministry, also falls to the ground.

With regard to the King's several Ministers plenipotentiary in India, what their powers were, or whether they had any powers at all, to authorize *such acts*, I will not pretend to say. These specific powers, never were produced. The King's Commissioners certainly never did act as principals; and however they might encourage, countenance, and even terrify the Presidency (as they state it) into the part they took against their judgment—they, as well as the Presidency, are parties, and cannot be witnesses. They, too, stand upon the truth of the facts which they alledge, of which they must bring proof. Indeed they alledge none upon their own knowledge, nor is it to be expected they should; For the records of the East India Company were not in the hands of the Commissioners, and they could have no personal knowledge of facts. They were strangers in India, and could take their line, both of facts and politics, only from the Nabob, and from the Company's servants: which throws the whole back on the original actors, the Nabob, and the Select Committee; the one of which was a party in interest, and the other, as we have seen, acted against their own sense of things. Indeed, whether we consider the subordinate acting, either of the King's Commissioners, or the Company's servants; either using force, or submitting to it; whether the one is to be blamed, or the other pitied, it is perfectly ridiculous to urge their own assertions in justification of their own conduct. Men's own declarations are the strongest evidence against themselves, but they operate as nothing in their favour.

The author, even when he goes higher than Servants or Commissioners, and states his records in proof of the opinion of the Company itself, does not perform a great deal more for the cause he espouses.—The Company's disapprobation, in some instances, of the conduct of the Rajah of Tanjore—their wish, that *when convenient* he may be *chastised*, and that the Nabob's *pretensions* against him may be rendered effectual,—all this is not in the least material to the single point to be proved.

If we were to admit that the Directors, in the accounts, upon which they founded their opinions, were not deceived, and that their desire of *chastising* the Rajah, and of enforcing the *pretensions* of the Nabob, were perfectly just;—yet *chastisement* does not imply *deposing*; and enforcing the Nabob's *pretensions* does not, by the terms, authorize making a *conquest*. If the author can shew, that any where in that correspondence, the Company's servants had first stated to their masters, that they thought it expedient to *dethrone* the King of Tanjore, and to deliver over both him and his people to the mercy of the Nabob, Mahomet Ali; and that *these* were the Nabob's pretensions, and their views; and if the Company had approved their measures, on that fair state of them, the papers would have been properly cited to prove the Company's approbation. The facts, on which that approbation was grounded, would, indeed, still demand a proof—but the fact of the approbation itself, however obtained, would have been established. But as matters now stand, there is not a syllable in those records (such records as they are) to the purpose for which they are quoted. The Presidency never (as I have just remarked) once acquainted the Directors with such designs of theirs, or such pretensions of the Nabob. The pretensions of the Nabob, on which the Company gave their opinion, were only, that the Nabob might receive the arrears of his Pishcush, and a reasonable sum towards the charges of the war with Hyder Ali. These pretensions, and these only,

were

were before the Directors, and these only they did or could authorize.

On this point, the Presidency are themselves so full and explicit, as to take away all possibility of pretence that the Directors had any thing else submitted to their deliberation; for the Presidency says expresly " That in the expedi-
" tion against Tanjore, the *declared purpose to the world*
" (whatever the latent purpose might be) was to call the
" King of Tanjore to account, and *not* to conquer him."
" * We have," say they, " *no cause to infer, from any orders*
" *we have received from the Company,* that they wish the
" fort and country of Tanjore were *conquered,* and the
" present possessor dispossessed; but, *on the contrary,* that
" they [the Directors] would not have either their posses-
" sions, or those of the Nabob, extended, or *the hereditary*
" *possessors of territories dispossessed*; but only that they should
" be reduced to such terms as may give safety to the Carnatic
" and † their own possessions."

Words cannot be more expressive of their own sense of the orders of the Directors; they state those orders, as directly prohibiting that very act, which the writer of the pamphlet asserts the Directors to have approved; they state such a prohibition, as the known standing policy of the Company. The reader's natural feelings on the unexampled boldness of such assertions will supersede the necessity of observations upon my part.

* Company's App. P. 970. † Company's App. P. 703.

But

But the Presidency went further: they not only entertained this sense of the orders of the Company, but *they explained it fully to the Nabob himself*, and gave him no hopes of his keeping any conquests they might make for him, other than provisionally, till the Company's further orders should be received.

When that Presidency meditated the expedition against Tanjore, in the year 1771, they wrote to the Directors, "that "they were in a state of *uncertainty of what measures they* "*should pursue*," that "* they were resolved to represent to "the Nabob, with all frankness and candour, that in case "the King of Tanjore shall refuse to pay an adequate "sum of money, and the conquest of the country be "thereupon judged necessary, any arrangements respecting "such conquest must be regarded as *merely temporary, un-* "*til the Company's pleasure shall be known*; whose orders "thereon, they observe to *him*, *must be implicitly obeyed by* "*their servants*." They further recite, "† the Committee's "*avowed knowledge* that the Company wish *not to subvert* "*the established government of* ANY *power*, with whom they "have political connexion. In case the Rajah be subdued, "it were better *to restore him*, or to place some more fit "person of his family in the government of Tanjore, upon "paying such Pishcush to the Circar as might be proper, "assigning a revenue for payment of charges of the expe-"dition, and for the maintenance of a garrison to be kept

* Company's App. P. 33.

† Company's App. P. 35.

"in

"in the town on the part of the Company, and alſo for "a ſufficient force to protect the country; or, if the above "be not agreeable to the Nabob, that the revenues ſhould "then be put under his direction; but that *the fort ſhould* "*remain in our hands*, and that both ſhould be conſidered "as depoſits, *till the Company's pleaſure ſhould be known*.

The record containing this account, which *this candid writer* has totally omitted, puts an end to all pretence of deceit on their Nabob, which is one of our author's principal grounds for re-inveſting him with the kingdom of Tanjore. The Nabob knew, (if his aſſociates ſpoke truth) from the beginning the terms upon which he was to undertake hoſtilities. Firſt, He knew that his poſſeſſion (if he was to poſſeſs at all) was to be but *temporary*, and ſubject to the Company's pleaſure. Secondly, It ſhews, that the Select Committee were perfectly apprized of the Company's * invariable ſentiments (ſo often over and over again urged upon them) againſt extending the Nabob's territories, and againſt ſubverting any eſtabliſhed government. It is, in fact, the conſtant burthen of their ſong for years together. By all this, the direct contrary of this author's poſition, "That the Company authorized the *conqueſt*, "and deceived the Nabob," is fully and clearly proved.

It is remarkable, that the very Select Committee itſelf, under whoſe auſpices the conqueſt for the Nabob was carried on, had been inſtituted for the expreſs purpoſe of reſtraining and checking ſuch conqueſts. They could not take

* Vide Company's Appendix, No. xx.

a ſingle

a ſingle ſtep towards conqueſts, in their capacity of a Select Committee, without knowing that in that ſtep they violated their duty.

Our author, in ſtating the paragraph of the Directors letter which reproaches them with this breach of their duty, is pleaſed to talk of the Directors, as if they had miſrepreſented their own orders; and that their ſervants were better judges of their intentions, than themſelves. The Directors ſay, "That "the eſtabliſhment of a Select Committee, in March 1769, was "profeſſedly with a view to the confining our influence and "poſſeſſions, and to retreating back within thoſe limits "which our Governor and Council had exceeded, by at- "tempting to extend the poſſeſſions of the Nabob of the "Carnatic."

Our author is pleaſed to ſtile it "palpable ſophiſtry, to in- "clude Tanjore in this order," becauſe (as he ſays) it applied only to the invaſion of Myſore; as if the prohibition was reſtricted to one particular conqueſt, and did not extend to every act for ſuch purpoſes, that could diſturb the peace of the Carnatic. Unluckily for this author, on this, as on moſt occaſions, the expreſſions of the Select Committee itſelf, contain a full anſwer to their advocate; for they ſtate their own "*avowed knowledge*, that the Company wiſh not "to ſubvert the eſtabliſhed government of ANY power with "whom they have connection." Thus the advocate is an- ſwered out of the mouths of his clients.

But if their advocate is not put to ſilence by the confeſſion

of

of his own clients, he will find that the prohibition of making conquests was so far from originating on account of the Mysore war, so far from being subsequent to it, and confined to that object, that the Directors, in their Letters to the Presidency, chiefly condemn that Mysore war itself, as totally repugnant to their prior, positive, and repeated orders, to their orders both ancient and recent *.

Before I conclude this my inquiry into the Considerer's allegation of the Company's authority for the act which they reprehend in their servants, I think it right to point out to the reader, their sense of the kind of information which they had received from those servants. That information became the source of all the opinions they could entertain, or orders they could give: and its fullness and fairness was the first duty of every one in employment under them. Before their approbation can be pleaded for the acts of their servants, those who alledge it ought to prove that they performed their duty. But, it is to be lamented that they constantly gave or withheld information, as best suited their own designs. They were taxed by the Directors with being disingenuous, so early as in their accounts of their war with Hyder Ali, and in the midst of that labyrinth of wars and negociations †, in

* Appendix, vol. 2, p. 521.

† 13 "We cannot take a view of your conduct from the commencement of your negociation for the Circars, without the strongest disapprobation; and when we see the opulent fortunes suddenly acquired by our servants, who are returned since that period, it gives but too much weight to the public opinion, that

in which they choſe to be engaged at that time, for the ſake of extending the domination of the Nabob of Arcot. They expreſs their diſpleaſure at the war with Hyder Ali, "as being aggravated by the diſingenuous manner, in which their affairs were repreſented in their advices"—"The unfair manner in which they ſtate their views and motives, ſo very different from the ſpirit of their proceeding"—"Their declarations of their intention to make peace with Hyder Ali on certain conditions, and their having reaſon to conclude, that they had before fully determined on his entire *extirpation*"—"That at the latter end of June, they had expreſſed themſelves averſe to a rupture with Hyder Ali, whoſe power they deemed a reſtraint on the Marattas, but before the year was cloſed, the depreſſion of his power became a principal object of their politics *." This diſingenuous ſort of proceeding, in ſpite of thoſe remonſtrances, was not only continued, but encreaſed, in the advices ſent of the proceedings againſt Tanjore.

that this rage for negociations, treaties, and alliances, has private advantage more for its object than the public good.

14. "We therefore direct you to form a Committee, to make a rigid ſcrutiny whether any, and what ſums have been received for that purpoſe from the Subah of the Deckan, or his miniſter or agents, in the courſe of theſe negociations. You muſt apply yourſelves to the Subah or his miniſters; and you muſt uſe every effort to get a ſight of the Deckan treaſury books, where the moſt authentic information will be had; and if you do not act herein with that ſincere deſire to bring out proof which the occaſion requires, you will incur our higheſt reſentment." General Letter, &c. Append. p. 520.—*It may eaſily be imagined, how far theſe injunctions were obeyed.*

* Appendix, p. 518, 521.

The Directors, after stating that the plan mentioned by the Presidency, of keeping the revenue of Tanjore as a deposit until the pleasure of the Company should be known, proceed thus: " * The above advices were communicated to us by the ship " Duke of Portland, and your conduct upon the occasion " received, as it justly merited, our entire approbation. " That ship sailed from Fort St. George the 23d of July, " 1771; but we find, that *the very next day*, the Nabob be- " ing desirous of accommodating matters with the King of " Tanjore, the majority of the Select Committee resolved, " That such negociations should *not be conducted by our* " *representatives, as* guarantees of the treaty of 1762, but " *be left entirely to the Nabob:* and we also find, that " though you wrote to us three days afterwards over land, " *you never suggested the least hint of having departed from your* " *former opinion.*"

" † In September, 1771, you inform the Nabob, that as " you were acting in support of his government, and partly " as guarantees of the treaty of 1762, whatever should be " taken from the King of Tanjore, whether forts, coun- " tries, money, effects, or military stores, *all should be left* " *at his disposal, together with the Rajah, his family, and* " *dependents, if they should fall into your hands.* The " 9th of October following you wrote to us by the Stag

* 36 Par. of Gen. Letter, dated 12th April, 1775. Appendix, vol. I. p. 147 and 148.

† 38 Par. Ditto.

" frigate,

" frigate, *but were entirely ſilent reſpecting the above ſtipu-* " *lations*; and as you thought proper to defer ſending us " your proceedings by that conveyance, we received a copy " of the treaty of 1771, *before* we were apprized of the " unwarrantable engagements entered into with the Na- " bob."

Here the reader will ſee, and will pity, the miſerable condition of the native Princes of India. At the ſame time he will ſee the neceſſity of not being too haſty in his credit to the Nabob's advocates, when they cenſure the Company for inconſiſtency of conduct, in their endeavours to rectify errors into which they may have fallen, by giving too eaſy a belief to their ſervants abroad, who have not ſcrupled to miſlead them by the moſt unjuſtifiable repreſentations.

The author of the work before us, who prides himſelf on his candor, ought to have taken ſome notice of the character given by the Directors of theſe repreſentations; but he has wholly ſuppreſſed it; as he has, indeed, ſuppreſſed moſt of the repreſentations themſelves. Theſe material circumſtances, ſo ſuppreſſed, entirely clear the point in queſtion; as they ſhew by what means, and to what objects, the Company's *entire approbation* was received.

Thus I have ſhewn the natural invalidity and incompetency of moſt of this author's evidence, being the *evidence of the parties themſelves*; I have ſhewn, that where it might be competent, it was not to the purpoſe; I have ſhewn that theſe parties (parties as they are) confeſs that they acted againſt their judgment, againſt their duty, and againſt the expreſs orders they received; and I have ſhewn that the approbation pleaded in their favour was obtained upon a premeditated concealment of the truth, and ſuggeſtion of falſhood.

SECTION III.

Examination of the motives to the war on the King of Tanjore, in 1771—*Our ſtate relative to the King of Tanjore and the Nabob of Arcot—Ambitious views of the Nabob, and his early deſign on Tanjore—War with Hyder Ali—Breach of the treaty of* 1771.

I Shall next beg leave, having reviewed the defence of this conqueſt ſo far as it is placed upon the ground of authority, to conſider it a little on the foundation of reaſon and juſtice.

To enter into a country with fire and ſword—to plunder it without mercy—to ſeize upon the perſon of a Prince—to confiſcate his revenues—to deſpoil him of all his effects, and to impriſon him and his family, are no light things; nor to be done but upon ſerious grounds, and the moſt urgent and evident neceſſity.—Some delay of payments (however juſt and reaſonable the demand) is no reaſon at all for drawing the ſword and throwing away the ſcabbard. It is not a want of ſtrict performance of every minute engagement;

engagement; it is not every charge of his having engaged in a ſcuffle with a neighbouring power (even if the charge were perfectly true, and the act not perfectly defencible) that can juſtify the invaſion of a country, and the total deſtruction of an illuſtrious family. Nor ought our Preſidency, in reaſon, conſcience, or policy, to have lent themſelves to ſuch enterprizes on ſuch grounds; even after they had embarked in the war, they themſelves declare to Mahomet Ali, their wiſhes that the matter might be rather terminated by a *negociation:* their wiſhes, therefore, whether real or pretended, indicate their judgment to be—that extenſion of conqueſt ought, if poſſible, to be avoided. They ſay, that they incline to think it not good policy to reduce Tanjore, and place it under the management and control of the Nabob.

So far, however, from trying the effect of negociation, though the King of Tanjore, both by his Letter and by his Vakeel, had declared himſelf ready and willing to ſettle every thing through the mediation of the Engliſh *, they

* Company's Appendix, p. 717. Minutes of Select Committee, 27th July, 1771. The Committee had recommended it to the Vakeel to go to the Nabob.—The Minute recites, "The Vakeel ſeemed much alarmed, ſaid, *his Maſter had, in his* "*Letter to the Preſidency, referred the differences between him and the Nabob, to the* "*Company, and wiſhed we would take upon us to mediate between them.*" Some time after, being again admitted, the Vakeel ſaid, "his Maſter was ready and "willing to ſettle terms of accommodation, under the guarantee of the Engliſh, "on whoſe faith and promiſe he would rely; but he would never truſt the Na-"bob, *without the ſecurity of the Engliſh,* as he well knew the Nabob's inten-"tions were to accommodate matters for the preſent, but that he had bad inten-"tions, whenever an opportunity ſhould offer in future."

 chofe

chose to follow the Nabob's advice, and, agreeably to their expressions, *to drive him to despair*.

From the resolution of driving him to despair arose those two cruel wars, which, within the compass of about two years, they waged upon the King of Tanjore. In the first of which, they weakened and exhausted that kingdom; in the last of which, they deposed the Sovereign, and ruined the country. The first of these invasions by the Nabob, was in 1771, the latter in 1773.

I shall endeavour to state, as shortly as possible, both the motives and the pretexts to those wars; and for this purpose it will be necessary, for the satisfaction of those readers who are not perfectly conversant with Indian history, to turn our eyes a few years backward.

When the Company first began to interfere in the politics of India, they found the then King of Tanjore an hereditary sovereign Prince, in undisturbed possession of great splendor, power, and opulence, derived from a long line of royal ancestors. Mahomet Ali, second in descent from an adventurer appointed to the Phousdary, or subordinate military government of Arcot, by the Subah or Viceroy of the Decan—and that, too, in prejudice of his *elder brother*, still living—was found by the Company, at that time, capitulating with his rival, Chunda Saheb, the protegeé of France, for his last fortress.

With Tanjore the Company formed the first regular alliance

 they

they made in India*; and by that alliance they instantly acquired an important place, the town and district of Devicota.—By the assistance of the King of Tanjore, they gave the first turn to the war with France. Mr. Lally was repulsed from the walls of Tanjore; the siege of which place had been undertaken, and its destruction denounced, for the King's adherence to our interests. Through the whole of that war, to the final reduction of Pondicherry, he assisted, with his troops, in the Common Cause.

The Nabob of Arcot had the largest, the most immediate, and the most beneficial share of all the strength he exerted. Tanjore first preserved him from Famine † in Trichinopoly; and afterwards continued a support to him, with so much steadiness and effect, that at length the General of that country, Monackagi, (one of the gallantest men, and one of the best officers that was perhaps ever born in India) delivered to him the head of his rival Chunda Saheb; and thereby put him in the undisputed possession of his governments. These are substantial and notorious facts, recorded in the histories of the Coromandel wars, before the present controversies had given occasion to alter, to colour, or to disguise them. The endeavour to weaken the force of these facts at this day, by a subtle discussion of the motives of the several actors at several periods, or by involving them in the

* Orme's Hist. and Appendix, Vol. I. No. 5.

† Nabob's Letter, March, 1775. "The support of the fort of Trichinopoly "depends on the friendship of the King of Tanjore and Tondeman."

intricate politics of India, will be of little avail to weaken the conclusions which naturally result from them. They stand, and will stand, as monuments to prove to the latest posterity, how much of our power in India has been owing to the favour and protection of a generous Indian Prince, whom, at that time, we did not disdain to call a King *, as he had always been called by ourselves and all the world, and to address him by the style of Majesty; though some have lately thought fit wholly to leave off that title and that mode of address; and can use no other names for him than *feudatory, vassal, zemindar*, and other contemptuous appellations; used indeed promiscuously, with little regard to their contradictions one to the other; but all of them contrary to his rights; and some of them used in a sense repugnant to any ideas hitherto entertained in India. The sense of some of those terms seems indeed to be very imperfectly, if at all, understood by those who have thought proper to apply them to this Prince.

The late King of Tanjore (father of the present) had at times his doubts and fears of those, whom upon the whole he faithfully supported; and it was nothing but what was very natural. If he had apprehensions from the power of France and Chunda Saheb, he had something likewise to dread from the English and from Mahomet Ali. Grounds for his apprehension had been furnished at a very early period

* Company's App. No. 3 and 4, and all the Correspondence from our first intercourse with him.

in our intercourſe; and bitter experience has ſince ſhewn him, that he was not wholly miſtaken.

Our acquaintance with the King of Tanjore began with an attempt to ſet up a pretender to his crown, and with hoſtilities commenced in conſequence of that attempt. The origin of our union with the Nabob was the very reverſe of this. Our connection with him began, by our freeing him from a powerful Rival and Pretender to his authority; if a man, almoſt in poſſeſſion of all, in actual poſſeſſion of Arcot, and by as good a title as his own, could be called a Pretender. But unfortunately, when power is in queſtion, it is better to receive than to confer benefits. The fate of the two allies has been in the inverſe proportion of their merits and ſervices. From ſtanding on the verge of ruin, from a ſtate almoſt of captivity, Mahomet Ali is become, by the aſſiſtance of the Engliſh and the King of Tanjore, one of the moſt powerful princes in India;—the King of Tanjore, from immenſe opulence, is now very nearly what the Nabob was found at the commencement of our connection with him. When the Engliſh firſt became acquainted with the King of Tanjore, they were ſo ſtruck with the magnificence of his court, that they thought it worthy of a particular notice. "On our entering *," ſays Colonel Lawrence "the Tanjore country, the King ſent his prime "miniſter, Succogee, to compliment the Nabob and his "allies.—On our arrival at Candore, the King deſired to meet

* Cambridge, Page 58.

"the

"the Nabob and me half way. I ſet out the 4th, in company with the Nabob and Mr. Palk, who had been with me from my leaving Madraſs. The King met us at the place appointed, attended by his whole Court, who on the occaſion made a very magnificent, ſplendid appearance. He was eſcorted by 3,000 horſe, well mounted, and a great many elephants in ſilver trappings. After ceremoniouſly paſſing each other in our palankeens, we were conducted to a pleaſant garden, and there received by the King, under a pavilion ſupported by pillars of ſilver, elegantly covered and furniſhed. There we renewed our aſſurances of friendſhip and protection, and all our former engagements; and it was determined that the King ſhould ſupport the Nabob, and join him the next day with three thouſand horſe, and a like number of ſeapoys. After a refreſhment of fruits, a ſhower of roſe water, and being anointed with otter of roſes, we were diſmiſſed with preſents of elephants, horſes and ſirpahs, and eſcorted to our camp by a brilliant party of the Rajah's cavalry."

It is not neceſſary to make the late forlorn, or even the preſent patched up condition of the Prince of that country, a contraſt to this deſcription; which however is far ſhort of what might in thoſe days be given, without exaggeration, of the ſplendour of the court of Tanjore, ariſing from the opulence of a territory, not great indeed in extent, but filled with a numerous, flouriſhing, well-governed, induſtrious and contented people.

This

This wealth of the kingdom and court of Tanjore, which at firſt excited admiration, came afterwards, probably, to ſtimulate other paſſions. The advantage which the Nabob derived from the uſe of part of it, became his motive for wiſhing to ſeize upon the whole. From the moment that the ſuperiority of the Engliſh forces in India was become indiſputable, and that he found means of acquiring ſuch an influence as to obtain the direction of thoſe forces, he began to form a variety of ambitious * deſigns, which were to be compaſſed by the deſtruction, or (according to his favourite expreſſion) by the *extirpation* of all the princes of that country. He even went ſo far as to propoſe a rebellion againſt his immediate maſter, the Subah of the Decan †; a power equally under the protection of that treaty of Paris, upon which his partizans affect excluſively to value him. This propoſition, of placing himſelf by rebellion on the ſeat of his ſuperior, had no other pretence, than the benevolent idea, that the diviſions of the Subah's family afforded him a favourable opportunity.

* After giving account of the ſurrender of Pondicherry, Mr. Orme gives the following lively deſcription of the avaricious, ambitious, and vindictive ſpirit of the Nabob: " The Nabob requeſted and *expected*, that the army, after the ne-" ceſſary repoſe, would accompany him againſt ſuch Chiefs and Feudatories " whom he *wiſhed*, or had pretenſions to call to account, either for contempts " of his authority, or for tributes unſettled or withheld. He had not for-" given the rebellion of his half-brother Nazeabulla of Nelore; his indigna-" tion had never ceaſed againſt Mortizally the Kellidore of Velore, and " Arielore and Worriorpollain to the South, were *ſuſpected of hidden trea-" ſures*; ſtill more the greater and the leſſer Maravars; *and the King of " Tanjore, wealthier than all, ſcarcely conſidered the Nabob as his ſuperior.*" Orme, Vol. II. Page 725.

† App. No. XX.

" The

" The tenor § of the Nabob's conduct" (say the Presidency who acted in support of that design) " points out clearly, that " the conquest of the Tanjore country, the Mysore pos- " sessions in the Payen Ghaut, and the possession of the De- " can, are objects of which his ambition has never lost sight."

Our author condescends to allow, that this project had found place in his mind, *" He wished to be made Subah " of the Decan. He did so. But when the Company wished " the contrary, observe (says his advocate) how this ambi- " tious aspirer expressed himself—† It is true, I was desir- " ous of extending my government and your influence " over the whole Decan country, but" (adopting, by the by, the very words of the Directors) " as a little in peace, and " security, is to be preferred to uncertain and greater pos- " sessions, involved in difficulties and so liable to troubles, " *agreeably to your friendly advice*, I shall confine my views to " peace and the Carnatic country, satisfied that I shall never " want your protection."

Though he missed the opportunity of gratifying his ambition, he furnishes matter of panegyric to our author, in the merit of relinquishing to the Directors, designs which he could have no shadow of hope of carrying into execution but by English forces. The intention being however substantiated, proves the extent of his ambition; which is all I have to do

§ Company's Appendix, Vol. II. P. 609.

* Considerations.

† Extract from Nabob's Letter to Directors, January, 1778, Pages 58, 59.

with it. The relinquiſhing of his object proves nothing more, than that he can ſubmit to neceſſity. No body ever doubted it. Indeed there is no one who will be at the pains to look through his correſpondence, but muſt ſee that it is his conſtant method to propoſe ſcheme after ſcheme, project after project, for raiſing diſturbances, and enlarging his power; and though he often lays thoſe projects down as lightly as he takes them up, he has, at the ſame time, the addreſs to make a merit of giving up one of his deſigns, to ſerve him in obtaining aſſiſtance for the execution of another.

Fruſtrated in his hopes of obtaining the Decan, he propoſed a plan for the *extirpation* of Hyder Ali, the Nabob of Myſore. He had the luck to engage the arms of the Company in this wicked ſcheme, contrary to all the ideas and inſtructions of the Direction. The author indeed, in juſtification of an attempt which ended in his patron's and our diſgrace, tells us, that * "The plan of conquer-"ing that *country*, *originated ſolely* with the Governor and "Council of Madraſs. It was a meaſure *certainly very im-"proper*; but of its impropriety, even in its commencement "or progreſs, much leſs in any *objects of ambition it was to "attain*, the Nabob had *no ſhare*, for he was *allured* into the "part he took in that tranſaction, by the *fallacious promiſes* "of the Company's ſervants, calculated to make him in-"ſtrumental to their purpoſes."

It is a little hard in the Nabob's advocate, to lean ſo heavily

* Conſiderations, Page 59.

heavily on his friends at Madraſs. I believe it would not be difficult to prove, that the meaſure originated in the Durbar, and not in the Preſidency; but our author and I agree that it was "*certainly a very improper meaſure.*" I ſhould not have quarrelled with him, had he uſed a ſtronger term: but where-ever it might originate, it was (had not the attempt failed) to have concluded, with putting the kingdom of Myſore into the poſſeſſion of the Nabob. A regiment of Europeans and ten thouſand Seapoys were to be kept up, to eſtabliſh him in that poſſeſſion. The author agrees that the Preſidency did hold out *ſomething* to him, and did make him *ſome promiſes.* He certainly claimed a right to Myſore; and the author tells us, that the Company cannot *conquer* for themſelves. * "The "East India Company are," ſays he, "a chartered body "of merchants united, as their appellation expreſsly im-"ports, merely for the purpoſes of trade. The powers "therefore with which they are inveſted, are limited to "the protection of their property and commerce; if they "tranſgreſs this line, and attempt, *as principals,* to con-"troul ſovereign Princes, *they aſſume a lawleſs power.*" None but the Nabob, according to his own ideas and thoſe of his advocate, could poſſeſs the country. I am therefore obliged to put the Myſore war to the account of his ambition; without meaning to exclude any other purpoſes, that the author may attribute to his aſſociates, who, it ſeems deluded him, or, to preſerve his own term as more expreſſive,

* Conſiderations, Pages 67.

allured

allured him with "fallacious promises." The truth however is, that their proceedings were in consequence of the Nabob's own proposals. *

Whatever were his designs on Mysore, or whoever may have allured him into them, Tanjore was the ultimate object of all his manœuvres, and that which he never suffered to escape out of his view. To that point the testimonies of the gentlemen concerned with him in the execution of these designs, are full and direct; for, besides what they have just told us, they further say, † "That the Nabob "has *constantly* had in view the design of *conquering Tanjore*, "*will not admit of a doubt*; and we are firmly persuaded, "that his chief motive for concluding peace with the "Rajah, at a time when our troops were upon the point "of getting possession of the place, arose *from his jea-* "*lousy, least the Company purposed, at a convenient opportunity,* "*to take the country from him.* By that expedition however "he obtained, what he *earnestly wished for, viz.* the *removal* "*of that restraint* which he thought himself under by the "*Company's guarantee of* 1762."

Here some very material points are settled on their proper basis. First we see established, the systematic design of the Nabob for the conquest of Tanjore, which shews that his quarrel was in subservience to that design, and not that design formed in consequence of any grounds of quarrel. In the next place, this passage proves, that his treaty of

* Company's Appendix, Page 521.

† Company's Appendix, Vol. I. Page 230. 521.

1762, and the Company's guarantee, were a great burthen to him; and consequently that all his allegations of breach of that treaty on the part of the King of Tanjore, must naturally be suspicious, where it was so much his interest and his wish to suppose it violated.

From that, his grand, original, invariable purpose of the conquest of Tanjore, he never ceased from the moment of his settlement in the Carnatic. He therefore never omitted any means to bring on a rupture with that kingdom †; for finding himself obliged to desist from his monstrous claim of exacting indefinite sums by force, and to accept of a certain payment with a positive exclusion of all other demands, by the *odious* treaty of 1762, he made perpetual efforts to set aside that agreement; first, on *his* usual pretence of having consented to it *unwillingly*, and afterwards by stating it as a temporary arrangement, which expired with *the* father of the present King of Tanjore. In pursuance of the same invariable purpose, he made a black attempt to accuse the present King of Tanjore of the murder of that father. That charge indeed he dropped, as soon as he found that the good sense and humanity of Mr. Palk discouraged so malicious and shocking an invention; and instantly relinquishing his accusation of poison and murder (with as much readiness as he abandoned the conquest of the Decan, and for the same reason) he wrote the King of Tanjore a congratulatory letter on his succession to the throne of his father, as false as the accusation he had

† Company's Appendix, Vol. I. Page 53.

began with. He has made, and to this hour continues to make, perpetual attempts to desolate * the country of Tanjore, by diverting the water which fertilizes it. Had he been suffered intirely to accomplish this latter scheme, it would have brought on a famine in that country, and even distressed the whole coast of Coromandel.

His continued hostile designs were evident; and in India he took no pains to conceal them. For a long time, however, he was not able, either by his numerous agents here, or by his manoeuvres at Madrass, to engage the English forces in a project so contrary to all decency, reason, policy, and public-faith. He was more early in his success in engaging them in the other and preliminary part of this plan, the extirpation of the King of Mysore, which I cannot avoid mentioning from its perpetual connection with the present question. He knew that if he succeeded in that part of his plan, that Tanjore would not be in a condition to give him a moment's opposition. Failing of the success he expected against Hyder Ali, he endeavoured to make himself amends by renewing his attempts on Tanjore itself. He now saw a most favourable opportunity. He saw, that the losses and expences of the Company in that Mysore war, would make

* Company's Appendix, P. 68. Nabob's Plea. "The banks of water "belonging to the Tanjore country remain in my bounds; for which reason "the affairs of Tanjore *can be finished in a better manner whenever we require.*" Nabob's Plea, P. 71. App. 5th Par. "In case of displeasure, if a few Cooleys "are sent to break down the banks, it occasions great loss to the Tanjoreans; "and the Tanjore country will be in great want of water."

 them

them readily liſten to any ſcheme againſt Tanjore, ſhort of conqueſt (the deſign of which he as carefully concealed from them, as he was indifferent about its publication in the Eaſt) that promiſed reimburſement of their charges. At the ſame time he knew that the Preſidency at Madraſs, loaded with the diſgrace and blame of that unfortunate and unprovoked attempt, would be very ready to lay the cauſe of failure any where rather than on themſelves, or on their aſſociate; and that of courſe they would be ready to join heartily in any complaint againſt a neighbouring power, the moment the circumſtances of the country would permit it. All theſe motives concurred to foment the quarrel with the King of Tanjore, which was ripened into a war in the year 1771 *.

* Conſider. P. 15, 16.

SECTION IV.

Pretexts for the war of 1771 examined—Duplicity of the Nabob and his Party.

THE above being the real *motives* to the war, namely, the ſettled ſyſtem of the Nabob for the conqueſt of Tanjore, and the neceſſity for finding ſome advantage to ballance the loſſes and diſgraces in the war with Hyder Ali; it is neceſſary to ſtate the *pretexts* for it, and to examine into their merits. The firſt of theſe pretexts was, That in this war with Hyder Ali, the Rajah had not ſent aſſiſtance to him (Mahomed) and the Preſidency of Madraſs.—The ſecond was,—that he had made war on certain Polygars under the Nabob's protection.—The Third,—that the ſtated payment of the Moguls's tribute, had been delayed beyond the uſual time. *

With regard to the firſt of theſe pretexts, the not ſending aſſiſtance in the war of Myſore with Hyder Ali,—let us ſuppoſe for a moment, that the charge was founded, and not one man had been ſent on the occaſion. Will Mahomed Ali's advocates condeſcend to ſhew what obligations the King of Tanjore was under, to take any part whatever in that war? The treaty of 1762, never bound him to any ſuch aſſiſtance; nay, it contained expreſs words, limiting the whole of his duty to the payment of the Mogul's tribute. This is confeſſed by the very ſame perſons who made war upon him for not ſending the aſſiſtance which he was not bound to ſend; for in the courſe of that war, they expreſsly tell the Nabob himſelf, " That as *no mention* is made in *any* part of the " treaty, that he, the King of Tanjore, is obliged to join us " on *any* occaſion, the Governor oppoſes making the de- " mand of money; eſpecially as his conduct ſince, has, in " ſome meaſure, made amends for it, *a body of his troops be-* " *ing now employed with Colonel Wood.* However, as the

* Vide Conſid. P. 15.

" Rajah

" Rajah will be *ſecure* in the peaceable enjoyment of his poſ-
" ſeſſions, the Governor agrees to *requeſt*, that he will bear
" a *further* part of the burthen of the war; but whether
" he *will voluntarily conſent thereto, may be* doubted; for as, by
" the treaty with him, we have deprived ourſelves of *every*
" *pretence* to *inſiſt* upon it, were we to make ſuch a demand,
" it might be conſtrued *a breach of treaty*, and bring *a re-*
" *proach upon your Excellency, as well as upon ourſelves, of a*
" *breach of our faith*; which, bound as we are by ſuch *ſolemn*
" *engagements*, we ought ſcrupulouſly to avoid giving the
" leaſt foundation for." *

So far as to the part the King of Tanjore was bound by treaty to take in that, or in any conteſt of the Nabob; and ſuch is the ſentence paſſed by the Preſidency on the firſt ground of their attack on Tanjore, I mean its not having aſſiſted in the war againſt Hyder Ali,—the merits of which war, at this day, no man (no not our author) attempts to juſtify, on the ground either of its juſtice or expediency; and in the event of which, there was ſo little reaſon for exultation. But whatever the merits of that war might be, ought we not to aſk, If the Rajah was not *bound* by treaty to aſſiſt in it, had he any other motives? Was he previouſly conſulted about it? Was he to derive any ſort of immediate benefit from it? Was it for his remote intereſts? On the contrary, was it not made for the direct purpoſe of deſtroying every power capable of keeping the Nabob of Arcot within the bounds of moderation, and

* Company's Appendix, P. 169.

conſequently

confequently of having the King of Tanjore entirely at his mercy? The very advocates for the Nabob tell us it was "a very improper meafure."—If it appears fo to them, what could recommend it to the Rajah?—had he embarked with zeal and eagernefs in fuch a war, he muft have been completely out of his fenfes.

The reader who finds, that the Rajah's holding back of affiftance in the war with Hyder Ali, is made a ground of war upon himfelf (though on fuch a foundation as we have juft feen) will be led to fuppofe, that the fact at leaft is indifputable. It is indeed a fpecies of fact, the exiftence or non-exiftence of which cannot be equivocal. What muft be the reader's indignation, when he fees in the paper juft cited, that the foundation of the charge is abfolutely falfe; and that the King of Tanjore, from his defire of being well with our nation, notwithftanding his well-grounded fear (and hatred, if you pleafe) of Mahomed Ali, actually did fend 3000 men to that war, under Colonel Wood? This is directly acknowledged in the fame letter of the Prefidency, from whence the laft extract is made.

The charge is made by the Nabob, and it is argued in the pamphlet before us, as if no affiftance at all had been fent; yet, as the fact to the contrary ftared them in the face, it was neceffary to difpute the *value* of the fervices; and without any attention to the contradiction, they affert, "That the Rajah's "troops were of no manner of ufe."

There is fo little dependence to be had upon affertions from

from the Nabob's quarter, and ſo little light has been thrown on the detail of that war, that I cannot undertake to ſay poſitively whether they were of uſe or not. It is not indeed eaſy to aſcertain the proportion of the utility of any particular corps of troops ſerving in a large army. Though the Commander may not employ them, they ſtill tend to give reſpect, and add to the opinion of the general ſtrength. If they were not employed, and ought to have been ſo, it was the fault of the Nabob and his Allies, who had the entire command of them, and who did not chooſe to employ them. But if from their ill conſtitution, or their diſaffection, they had been (which I take to be far from the caſe) of no uſe; yet let it be recollected that they could not be more defective than the Nabob's * own troops, who were *worſe* than of *no* uſe; for if they did not abſolutely betray the places they were appointed to garriſon, to Hyder Ali, they abandoned them through cowardice and want of diſcipline, and thus became one cauſe of the unfortunate iſſue of that unjuſt war.

But if the Nabob's friend takes new ground, and will

* Our author himſelf gives us his unqueſtionable teſtimony to the badneſs of the Nabob's forces. He does not ſuppoſe that the Nabob would wiſh to truſt even his darling prey of Tanjore in the hands of his own forces. "He muſt," (ſays his advocate) "well remember the danger of Trichinopoly, which "would have fallen into other hands, if the troops of the Company had not "been within its walls; that if Tanjore were only defended by the Nabob's "ſeapoys, a ſudden attack upon it by the European powers, and other enemies, "might loſe that country to the Nabob, and involve in conſequence, both "him and the Company in heavy misfortunes." Conſiderations, P. 61.

aſſert

assert that the *delay* and not the refusal of sending troops was made the cause of complaint; to this I answer, that when the fact of his sending troops is established, when it is proved that he was under no obligation to furnish any troops, I have a right to ask, how his delay in sending what he was not obliged to send at all, should become a crime of that magnitude?

But I will suppose, for argument, that he was obliged by some duty or other, to send a military force in this (to him unnatural) war; yet, as no treaty had either defined the time, nor the * quota, nor had any specific requisitions been made, how came the late time and deficient quantity of the

* "What *quota* of troops or treasure should be furnished in time of war, we "*cannot ascertain*, either *by usage or compact*; it appears therefore to us, to have "been *arbitrary*: that is to say, the government of the Carnatic hath *exacted* "*whatever it had power to compel, and Tanjore hath refused succours or money, as far* "*as the government thought it had power to support such refusal.* As this is by no "means peculiar to these two states, the same principle prevails invariably "throughout Indostan." Appendix, P. 938.

N. B. This is a testimony from an enemy. The Presidency recommending the reduction of Tanjore for the benefit either of the Nabob or the Company, on the same mere principle of *power and policy*, without a pretence of *right*—it may possibly be matter of curiosity to the reader to see what the conclusion is that they draw from the above premises. "Upon this principle (say they) which "*is wholly that of power*, it is certainly contrary to the sound policy of the Car- "natic to suffer the *existence of such a state.*"—*Viz.* Tanjore. To common men it would seem an odd conclusion, that because a foreign state *claimed* an extravagant and absurd *power* over another state, therefore the state that was vexed by the exercise of that power, ought *not to be suffered to have existence.* It would, to plain sense, sound as well, that since so absurd a power was vexatious and mischievous to humanity, the *power* ought to be annihilated, and *the state* over which it was claimed, set free from the vexation of such monstrous pretensions.

H aid

aid he sent, to become a just ground of hostility against him? The confederates make no scruple to receive and derive all the advantages they could from the King of Tanjore's troops, (which they confess they had no right to require); and when they have no longer occasion for them, and have clapped up a peace with their enemy, then they fall upon their ally, on the pretence of his not having done enough.

Let us however go the full length they would have us go, and admit the delay and its guilt in the fullest extent, yet surely it is not decent for those to complain of the delay of others, who are not alert themselves. The Nabob, who thinks the Rajah's delay a good reason for making war upon him, was himself slow enough to take the field against Hyder Ali. That very Presidency, who joined him in making war upon Tanjore, on pretence of remissness, express their sense of his own conduct in this affair in the fullest and strongest manner. After charging him with being himself the occasion of the abortion of all his own designs, and with his failure in all his engagements, they accuse him of "the "*non-payment of his arrears to his own horse*, which had been a "*long time lying inactive, and refusing to act for want of pay*— "the Nabob (say they) after *his* proposal of going to camp, "was *often pressed to do so*, and to put his horse in motion; but "he could *not be prevailed on to stir*, nor did *any* of his horse "move from Arcot *until a few days before Hyder's arrival at* "*the Mount*;" * that is to say, at the gates of Madrass, where

* Company's App. P.

he

he and they were obliged to ſubmit to the terms of the conqueror. If the Nabob could not be prevailed on to bring his force into the field until the laſt moment, although in his own cauſe, where his glory, his intereſt, and all the great prizes of his ambition were at ſtake, and that too againſt the object of his bittereſt enmity, with what face could he reproach, much leſs make war upon the King of Tanjore, for want of alacrity in a war calculated, in the ſecond remove, for his own deſtruction?

In the black annals of political perfidy, there are few inſtances to be found of ſo vile a proceeding, as the whole of this tranſaction; that is, the acceptance of the ſervice; the ſubſequent quarrel for not having received it; and, laſtly, a war made to puniſh the remiſſneſs of an ally, where the principal could not be perſuaded to ſtir.

If any thing could add to the horror and baſeneſs of it, it was, that the Preſidency had actually included the Rajah in the treaty of peace with Hyder Ali. They make a ſtudied merit with the Rajah, of having done ſo; though at home they tell another ſtory, and declare, that it was not done at their requiſition, but at that of the King of Myſore, who dictated the peace. But from whatever motive it was done, done it was; and it muſt have wiped off all the delinquency of the Rajah, if any ſuch had exiſted. This is the fact, and thus they ſtate it. The *manner* however in which the effect of this treaty is eluded in the pamphlet before us, is ſo very extraordinary, that I think I ſhall not be blamed for reſting

 a little

a little upon that part of the ſubject. I will therefore ſet out with ſtating it according to their own ideas of the tranſaction, and in the way they wiſh to have it underſtood.

*" By this treaty of 1769 (ſays the author of the pamphlet before us) " a new alliance was formed; to which however Hyder Ali would not accede, unleſs the *Rajah* of " Tanjore ſhould be included as a party to be protected. By " complying with his requiſition, and ratifying it in *favour* " of the Rajah, the Company *annulled the treaty* of 1762. The " Nabob *refuſing* to ſubſcribe this convention with Hyder, " he remained in his priſtine *ſituation*, conſidering himſelf as " *an ally only* of the Company."—† " For, beſides the new " relation now eſtabliſhed between the powers of Indoſtan, " whereby Hyder Ali became guarantee of the Rajah; " *not againſt the Nabob*, for he refuſed to ſign that in- " congruous convention, but *againſt the Engliſh*; the point " inſiſted upon by Hyder, that his Ally, the Rajah, ſhould " now be included as *a party to be protected*, addition- " ally proves, that his former protection under the former " guarantee had ceaſed."—‡ " A ſeries of cauſes concur to " deſtroy the treaty of 1762. It was *firſt* broken through " by the *repeated* perfidious conduct of the Rajah; it was " again annulled by the new treaty of 1769."

The game they play is perfectly new, and well worthy the attention of a reader, who may be inquiſitive to know the

* Conſid. Page 9. † Ibid. Page 37.
‡ Ibid. Page 40.

spirit

ſpirit of Britiſh oriental politics. The gentlemen at Madraſs make a treaty of peace with Hyder Ali, which includes the King of Tanjore. According to the letter and ſpirit of that treaty, it is admitted, that he ought to be ſafe and ſacred *as to them*. But then they have *an Ally*, the Nabob, in petto, who is *not included in the treaty*; he remained ſnug, and altogether unaffected by what had happened. "The Nabob * (ſays our author) refuſing to ſub-"ſcribe this convention with Hyder, he remained in his "*priſtine ſituation*, conſidering himſelf only *as an Ally* of "the Company," and the Company's convention was only "*againſt themſelves*, and not againſt the Nabob." The Nabob is therefore ſtill at liberty to fall upon the King of Tanjore; though that unfortunate Prince, who muſt be ſacrificed at any rate, had made war on the Nabob's own ſide, and was included in a treaty of peace, of which the Nabob had the full benefit.

Thus far Mahomed has taken his poſition with judgment. The Engliſh too are not ſo much hampered as may appear at firſt view. They come into play in their turn. Although we, *on our part*, are indeed bound by the treaty; though we tell the King of Tanjore that he owes his being included in it to *us*, yet *we* are at liberty (always, however, as allies to the Nabob) to join in the invaſion of his kingdom. That is, in other words, the Nabob, as *our* ally, is not bound

* Conſid. P. 9, and again P. 37.

by

by our treaty;—and as *his* ally, we are not bound by our own.

In this ſcandalous ſhuffle of prevarication and mutual connivance; by ſometimes appearing as principals, ſometimes as allies; ſometimes the Nabob being bound, and we looſe, and ſometimes the Nabob looſe, and we bound, this extraordinary confederacy has made ſport of the faith of the Britiſh nation, and of all faith.

But this is not the whole effect of the ſervice done the King of Tanjore by this treaty with Hyder Ali, which the Preſidency of Madraſs have, as they tell him, negociated in *his favour*, in 1769. It was not enough that that treaty laid him open to the hoſtilities of the Nabob, with the treaty-makers for his allies, but it had, it ſeems, as we have juſt read, an operation to annul all the former treaties, and particularly that of 1762.

If the annihilation of the treaty of 1762, was the conſequence of the King of Tanjore's being included in the treaty of 1769, why did not the Preſidency, who made ſuch a *merit* of including him in it, apprize him a little of the nature of the favor they had conferred on him? It was rather unkind to conceal from him the *full extent* of the obligation for which they claim his gratitude; and if he did not make all the return that was expected, it was probably from this their indiſcreet concealment of the value of the benefit.

But

But after paying our due homage to this ſingular act of friendſhip, it may not be improper to enquire a little into the validity of it: I ſhall therefore beg leave to aſk the gentlemen, on what principle the King of Tanjore, by being included by the Preſidency of Madraſs in the treaty of 1769, with Hyder Ali, came to forfeit the benefit of the treaty of 1762 with Mahomed Ali, and the guarantee of that treaty by the Company?—To ſhew that the latter of theſe inſtruments does really derogate from the former, ſo as to annul it, they are bound to produce this exterminating treaty of 1769, which devours every other, and to ſhew that it is contradictory to, and deſtructive of the firſt. If any thing could at this time of day be aſtoniſhing in this proceeding, it would be aſtoniſhing to obſerve, that the Nabob's partizans have neither produced this treaty, nor any one ſingle article, or part of an article in it; and yet they have the confidence to aſſert, that it annuls the treaty of 1762. I do not find it ſo much as contended for, that the treaty of 1762 was ever mentioned in that of 1769 *, or that one of the parties, Hyder, ſo much as knew of it; or that it had in any way ever become an object of the preceding negociation. It is indeed impoſſible to conceive, how a treaty of peace and mere indemnity with a third

* The treaty of 69 is to be found in the Book of Treaties publiſhed by the Company, Page 58. Although the Nabob is not mentioned perſonally in this treaty, his country, the Carnatic Payen Ghaut, is included in it; and the King of Tanjore is mentioned as a friend and ally of that country and the Engliſh Company.

2 perſon,

perſon, to which the Nabob (if we believe his advocate) was no contracting party, would annul a ſolemn treaty ſigned by himſelf.

As to the Engliſh, the reader will recollect, that the treaty of 1762 was made under the mediation, and with the expreſs guarantee, of that Preſidency of Madraſs which included the King of Tanjore in the treaty of 1769; it was approved and ratified by the Company at home; it was as complete a treaty as the Company could make it. Even if the advocates for the acts of that Preſidency were able to ſhew (what they never can ſhew) that the ſecond treaty which they made, contained matter derogatory to, and ſubverſive of the firſt, which was alſo made by themſelves, it could not excuſe, but would rather aggravate their perfidy. They were certainly not at liberty by their own poſterior voluntary act, to overturn their own prior engagement; or if they could, how can they have the abſurdity and effrontery to aſſert, that a treaty which gave to the King of Tanjore an *additional* ſecurity by including him in it as their *friend and ally*, was a deſtruction of the original ſecurity given by a former treaty?

The ſituation of the Princes of the Eaſt, in their dealings with the Nabob and his aſſociates, is frightful. Obſerve the ſituation of the parties before and after this treaty of 1769 with Hyder Ali. The Company, the Nabob, and the King of Tanjore, had been making a war on this Hyder Ali, with different intereſts, and (as the charge is) with different exertions. A peace is to be made. In that peace, what is

to

to become of the King of Tanjore? Is he to be included or not? If he is not, he is ſtill open to hoſtility from Hyder Ali, if Hyder Ali ſhall ſo chooſe; but if he is included in a common treaty, this is the worſt of all; for then according to their reaſoning and practice, the old treaty of 1762, the ſole baſis of all his ſecurity, is annulled; the guarantee is gone; and the Nabob, with the Company's forces in his train, falls upon him, unprotected by all guarantees, treaties, or alliances.—Thus no ſecurity whatſoever, joint or ſeparate, old or new, is valid in his favour; and ſuch are the principles of juſtice, of national honour, and of fidelity to engagements of thoſe who have the confidence to talk of public faith.

Having thus diſpoſed of the firſt ground of juſtification of the invaſion of Tanjore, by the faction of Mahomet Ali, in 1771, I paſs to the ſecond reaſon aſſigned for their violence, namely,—The non-payment of the Piſhcuſh *, or tribute money, due to the Mogul for his uſe, and payable through the hands of Mahomet Ali by the treaty of 1762.

On this, as on the former charge, the fact of the refuſal ſhould be firſt ſettled; becauſe it is the foundation of the whole complaint: but, as uſual with the Nabob's friends, no ſuch proof is attempted. *Some delay* of payment there

* Conſid. P. 64. " It deſtroys what ought to be their deareſt, as it is their moſt eſſential conſideration, *their Public Faith.*—Is private credit ſacred?—certainly and neceſſarily ſo:—On the ſame principle, but infinitely a larger ſcale, *ought Public Faith to be preſerved inviolate.*

certainly was; which, on comparing circumſtances, as well as they can be diſcovered through the Nabob's fraudulent relation of the matter, could not be above three months at the utmoſt beyond the ſtated time.—The King of Tanjore never denied the Mogul's tribute to be due. All he claimed was ſome remiſſion, or at leaſt a reſpite of payment; and he claimed it upon the following facts and principles:

Firſt, That he had ſent aids in the war of Hyder Ali, to the Nabob and the Company, at a very heavy charge, which had exhauſted his treaſures *.

Secondly, That his country had been eaten up by the emigration of vaſt multitudes of Mahomed Ali's ſubjects from Trichinopoly, and the adjacent parts for twenty country leagues, who fled from the ſuperiority of the Myſorean army, and were maintained in his country, and at his expence §.

Thirdly and laſtly, The Rajah alledged, that he was entitled to ſome allowance; as the country of Tanjore was, without any quarrel of his own, waſted by Hyder Ali, whoſe evacuation of it, he was obliged to purchaſe with a very heavy ranſom †.

Theſe were the grounds upon which the Rajah requeſted ſome abatement of his payments. The requeſt was plauſible if the allegations were true; and they formed a very juſt claim for ſome ſort of indemnification.—If not true, it behoved Mahomet Ali to ſhew the falſhood of them; it behoved the Preſidency, as guarantees of the treaty of 1762,

* Company's Appendix, P. 564 and 567. § Ibid. P. 614. † Ibid. P. 615.

 and

and if not as guarantees, yet as men of principle and common equity, to examine into the matter. All the anſwer the Nabob condeſcends to give, with regard to the firſt demand, is, " That it is not the uſage of India, for ſuperiors, " when followed by their inferiors in war, to make any " allowance or abatement in tribute for ſuch extra-ſervice."

To the ſecond head, of the maintenance of his refugees, he makes no anſwer at all.

As to the laſt, he thinks that as the Rajah has found ſo *much to pay to an enemy,* he ought *to pay a great deal more to a friend.*

To conſider the Nabob's firſt plea, the uſage of India, to make no abatement in tribute for extra-ſervices. The direct contrary being alledged by the King of Tanjore, and this being one of the points in iſſue, the Nabob ought to have proved his plea. An uſage which contradicted a principle ſo very conſonant to juſtice and reaſon, ought to be made perfectly clear before a war is to be undertaken on the ground of ſuch a cuſtom. But the Nabob never pretended to prove it, and was never called upon to prove either that or any thing elſe; his deſires were always regarded as reaſons, and his aſſertions were always conſidered as evidence. But the matter is ſtill worſe, for they receive the Nabob's aſſertions as proofs, even where they do not themſelves ſo much as pretend to give credit to them. It is with pain I find myſelf obliged to recite the manner of proceeding, and the opinions of that Preſidency, on the merits of their own

 war,

war, made in ſupport of the Nabob's extraordinary claim, to refuſe payment for the ſervices he receives. * "This *may* be "true (ſay they) though it is aſcertained by *no better teſti-* "*mony than the Nabob's.* We believe it *to be the cuſtom to* "*allow* Batta *even* to the troops of thoſe Rajahs and "Polygars *who are in abſolute ſubjection.*" They have, according to themſelves, nothing in favour of the claim but the Nabob's aſſertion; the contrary of which they believe to be true, even where the parties are in abſolute ſubjection, which they more than inſinuate not to be the ſituation of the King of Tanjore. †

On the ſecond head, of the King of Tanjore's countercharge, I have juſt obſerved, that as the Nabob had given no explanation, none was called for; ſo that on all European rules of evidence, the ground of the King of Tanjore's demand, on account of the expence of maintaining ſuch immenſe bodies of the Nabob's fugitive ſubjects, is perfectly eſtabliſhed, and he ought to have had full credit for it.

As to the third head, of the King of Tanjore's countercharges—His forced payment to Hyder Ali, and his loſſes from that invaſion—no attempt being made to deny or to evade this any more than the ſecond allegation, inſtead of its being made a pretext for hoſtility, it ought to have been

* Company's Appendix, P. 939.

† The King of Tanjore had, ſome years before, received an allowance for part of his charges at Maduſa. The prince of Tondé had received the ſame, by the Nabob's confeſſion. The uſage was, undoubtedly, the very reverſe of his ſtate of it.

admitted as a ground of repayment, or allowance in account. " He did" * say the Presidency (in a style of crimination) " fur- " nish provisions and pay a sum of money to Hyder, when he " entered the Carnatic in the beginning of 1769. But in this " he did *no more than other Polygars, who paid money to save* " *their particular districts from ravages, and which has not been* " *alledged against them as a crime.*"—The conclusion which they draw from hence is striking:—" *However, we have not* " *been influenced in his favour by any of these considerations*; and " have sufficiently explained in other places, our intention of " calling him to account *at a proper and safe time.*" It is their opinion, That because the King of Tanjore has been compelled to pay great sums to enemies, not of his own, but of the Nabob's creating, he therefore ought, *a fortiori*, to to pay larger sums to the Nabob himself as a friend. His extreme pride, insolence, and levity, towards a sufferer, from the effects of his unjust wars and wanton ambition, manifested in this reasoning, render him undeserving of any sort of answer, though very deserving of the most extreme punishment;—but our punishments are reserved for some thing else than delinquency.

But let us suppose the Rajah entitled, on a scrutiny, to no indemnity; yet, who has ever heard, before the date of this cruel and perfidious transaction, that war has been made on any power, because he had remained some short space, in arrear of a payment, offering at the same time to set it off,

* Company's Appendix, P. 685.

by

by countercharges to ten times the amount of the ſum deſired to be abated, and when the truth of no one of theſe countercharges had been ſo much as diſcuſſed? A mere delay on ſuch grounds could not be a crime, unleſs all diſcuſſion, and all attempts at an account, are crimes.

The King of Tanjore had hitherto, for a very great part of the time, been tolerably punctual in his payment; he had ſometimes even paid in advance; this he alledged, and his allegation was never denied. A perſon who ſometimes pays in advance, is fairly entitled in his turn to a reſpite; and rigour with him is unpardonable. Mahomet Ali ought to have conſidered his own caſe. He was himſelf a debtor *. So far from having paid his debts by advance to the Company, he had, in the courſe of the tranſaction received a thouſand remonſtrances on his delays; nay, he has gone ſo far as to declare, that in caſe of any troubles in his country he would make no payments at all. No troubles, however, in a country, no loſſes, no ſufferings, are pleadable against *him*. But Mahomet Ali is entitled to that equity which he has denied to others. Would all his reiterated delays and ſquabbles, and the diſcuſſion of ſo many accounts for ſo many years, have juſtified the making war upon him, and depoſing him? certainly not. Nobody ever contended for ſubjecting him to a rule ſo rigorous, though of his own making.

But there were other conſiderations, which, if not with

* "Above 30 lacks of principal money, which they (the Company) hazarded for his ſafety, and the defence of his government." Company's App. P. 687.

him,

him, ought to have had weight with the English in his interest. The Company had been themselves in the situation with regard to the Rajah, in which the Rajah stood with regard to the Nabob: they had agreed to pay a pishcush or tribute to the King of Tanjore, for the town of Devicota. It was, besides, in comparison of the importance of the object, but small. This pishcush however, they had not only not paid in advance, but were at one time five years in arrear. What was their conduct to the Rajah, and his to them, on that occasion of our delay of payment to him? Without pleading great expences and losses in his wars, and indeed without any plea, instead of paying their arrear, they request a discharge from him of the whole obligation. Did the Rajah make war upon them for this? The Rajah very kindly and gracefully gives them an immediate acquittal of the tribute for ever. "* As you solicited very much to be excused paying the "pishcush concerning Devicota, and as I esteem the Company's friendship to be best; and in order that the amity "and union between them and my government may, in a "perfect manner, be established on a firm and lasting footing, I have, agreeable to your desire, consented that the "said pishcush be remitted." This was the language of the King of Tanjore to the Company, then his debtor.

If the very ideas of equity, gratitude, and even common decency, had not been driven from our whole conduct in India,

* Company's Append. P. 43. King of Tanjore's Letter to the Presidency, Nov. 4, 1764.

some

ſome degree of ſhame and compunction muſt have ariſen at the recollection of this act of generoſity, when, to gratify the avarice and ambition of others, and perhaps our own, a civilized nation made ſuch haſte to pillage the goods of their neighbour and benefactor, and to ſpill the blood of their innocent fellow-creatures;—but there is more than enough ſaid on ſo very clear a point.

There remains only to examine the laſt pretext for this inhuman quarrel;—That the Rajah had made war on the Princes or Polygars of Marawar and Nalcooty; perſons dependent (as he alledged) on the Nabob of Arcot.—The fact of the Rajah's having made war on thoſe princes, is true. But have thoſe who make it a charge, attempted to ſhew that he was unjuſt and unreaſonable in that war?—not a ſingle word on the ſubject.

It is a right inherent in every ſovereign power, to ſeek redreſs by arms from thoſe who, he conceives, have injured him. The ſovereignty of the King of Tanjore is admitted by the Preſidency themſelves, even ſo late as in their conſultation of 16th November 1772. In the debate on the Nabob's titles, they ſay, * " That the Rajah of Tanjore, till his " late humiliation [in 1771] certainly never conſidered him-" ſelf as a *dependent* on the Nabob; he held himſelf *equal to* " *him at leaſt*. He paid, tis true, an acknowledgement " yearly *to the Empire*, but conſidered the Nabob as " no more than the *deputy*, the *officer of that empire*,

* Company's Appendix, Vol. I. P. 479.

authorized

" authorized to receive that acknowledgment; while he, the " Rajah, held his kingdom *by inheritance*, and exercised every " act of *independent sovereignty* in it. It might rather have " been expected, that he would have assumed a character of " *superior* dignity to that of the Nabob, whose office is con- " stitutionally revocable at pleasure."

The King of Tanjore had been, long before the date of that recognition of his independence, stated by the Presidency (that is in their Letter to the Nabob of 31st May 1762) * as a sovereign Prince. The Nabob himself admits it in his answer; repeating verbatim the very words of the letter, and agreeing to act in conformity to the advice given in consequence of the principle of sovereignty then stated to him from Madrass. It is thus expressed in his own letter: † " As the King of Tanjore is *a sovereign Prince*, it is " neither your interest nor mine to enter into a war, and that " you intend *therefore* to act as a *mediator* between us; desir- " ing me at the same time to look upon Mr. Dupre as your " representative, and give him the necessary instructions; *all* " *which I observe very fully*. Mr. Dupre having arrived here, " *informed me very fully* of your message. As you are my friend " in every respect, I regard your advice to be best; for which " reason I have wrote a letter to the King of Tanjore ex- " actly to the form inclosed."

Thus the sovereignty of the King of Tanjore is established beyond a doubt, by the confession of those who acted against

* Company's Appendix, Vol. I. P. 59. † Ibid. P. 61.

him, and even by the confeſſion of the Nabob himſelf; and of conſequence he had a right to do himſelf juſtice.

But he was a party in the cauſe, ſay the gentlemen of Madraſs, and ought not to act as a judge in it. It is not neceſſary to prove to theſe gentlemen, that to be at once a judge and a party, though incompatible with a ſtate of ſubjection, is an incident inſeparable from ſovereign power.—It is natural to aſk, what treaty or what law derogated from his ſovereignty, and hindered the King of Tanjore from righting himſelf on his neighbours? So far from being reſtrained by the treaty of 1762, it was then provided, that he ſhould be at full liberty to act againſt certain Polygars, not indeed there named, but who could be no other than thoſe in queſtion; as with them alone he had any diſcuſſion. The Nabob himſelf (the ſtanding evidence againſt his own pretenſions) ſome years before, and that too with great earneſtneſs, actually applied to the Preſidency, and intreated (for many good reaſons which he aſſigns) that thoſe Polygars might have no manner of protection. * "This day, being Thurſday "the 20th March, *Manozey* [the King of Tanjore's mi-"niſter) and *Tondeman*, have ſent their Vakeels, and with "a *great deal* of *diſpleaſure* have acquainted me in the man-"ner following, viz.

"We have been *your Allies from a* long *time*, and exerted "ourſelves to the utmoſt *in the time of the troubles*; we "uſed our endeavours, and *ſupplied* the *fort with proviſions* "*with very great pain and trouble*, in return for which you

* Company's Appendix, Vol. I. P. 39 and 40.

 "have

" have protected the Marawar (against our interest) and
" hindered us from *retaking the district, which he had possessed,*
" *to the prejudice of our honour.* If so, we shall be under the
" necessity of joining the Mysorean, to do what we can, and
" *to quit our alliance with you.* Should the Circar troops, or
" those of the English, assist the Marawar, we shall *be obliged*
" *to fight them.*"

After reciting this spirited message, which had very little the style of subordination, much less subjection, the Nabob proceeds: " I must observe to you, that the King of Tanjore
" and Tondeman are *neighbours* * to the fort of Trichino-
" poly, who *both assisted with provisions in the time of the war*
" *and troubles,* which supported the people in the fort. If
" we act the part of an enemy against them, it will be
" attended with a difficulty to defend the fort, *as we shall*
" *not be able then to get even a grain of provision, which will*
" *render me unable to reside here with my family. I have before*
" *and now,* wrote to Colonel Heron on this head to the
" following purport:

" The Marawar acted as *an enemy* for these five or six years
" past—we never reaped any advantage from him—we should
" not lose the King of Tanjore and Tondeman by giving
" our protection to the Marawar; *the support of the fort of*
" *Trichinopoly depends upon their friendship.*

" I am sensible that your order will be obeyed, and there-
" fore made bold to trouble you with this, hoping that you
" will write to the Colonel as soon as possible, *to quit his*

* Not dependents on it, as he afterwards thought proper to assert.

" *protection to the Morawar*, and to ſettle Tinnevelly. If the " Morawar joins the French and the Myſoreans, it is no " matter, for we can receive the Circar's money of him at " another time, or the King of Tanjore will anſwer for it. " The reaſon of my taking ſo *great care to avoid the animoſity* " *of the King and Tondeman, is*, that formerly the country of " Trichinopoly remained in our poſſeſſion; then we had no " occaſion to expect proviſions from other diſtricts, but now, " as the Myſorean is in poſſeſſion of the ſaid country, we " muſt *depend* upon theſe, viz. The King of Tanjore and " Tondeman's *friendſhip* for proviſions. I acquainted you " with what I thought was proper advice. My hope and " dependence is on your honour; you will do whatever may " be beneficial to me." *

By this letter (and it is not the only letter to the ſame effect) we ſee the Nabob not only conſenting, but moſt deſirous and earneſt, that no protection ſhould be given to the Marawar Princes. He recites the complaints of the King of Tanjore and Tondeman, which are in an high ſtyle of *diſpleaſure*. Not a word, not a hint, either on their part, or on the Nabob's, of any ſort of dependency or ſubjection. Their connection is treated by them, and not controverted by him, *as an alliance* only, which they threaten to withdraw from him, in caſe of his continuing to aſſiſt their enemies. This aſſiſtance, it muſt be remarked, he does not deny to have

* In the correſpondence, Comp. App. No. V. much more appears, which ſhews how much the Nabob encouraged the King of Tanjore in his pretenſions on the Marawar.

given,

given, notwithſtanding the obligations conferred on him by the King and by the Polygar of Tondeman, which he here acknowledges, and which he is ſo much in dread of not receiving in future, on account of his treacherous behaviour. Afterwards, when the Nabob, in that ſeries of wars made for him by the Company, undertook an expedition againſt Madura, (which by the way he afterwards declared to be undertaken * " without the leaſt reaſon,") † " At that time " the Nabob *requeſted* Monagee, General to the King of " Tanjore, to aſſiſt him in his expedition, and *deſired* the " General to defer his deſign until that affair was over, and " *then to clear his country.*" To this end he alſo prevailed on Mr. Lawrence to intercede in his favour.

Here the Nabob not only knows of the war of the King of Tanjore againſt the Polygars, but conſents to it; he acknowledges its juſtice by calling the territories in diſpute *his* [the King of Tanjore's] *country*, and the operations for obtaining them *clearing* it: and he only begs that expedition to be poſtponed on account of the aſſiſtance he himſelf deſired, and which he is ſo far from thinking himſelf entitled to command by his authority, that he calls in the aid of Mr. Lawrence's intereſt to obtain it.

Although the Nabob thought fit to deſiſt, or to appear to deſiſt for a time from his treacherous management with the Polygars, we find him purſuing the ſame clandeſtine courſe to incite theſe Polygars to hoſtilities, at the very time that he was preparing to make war on the King of Tanjore for

* Company's Append. P. 1507. † Ibid. 681.

having

having a quarrel with them. * "He proposed that we should "disband some of our Seapoys, to the end they might be "*secretly* enlisted by the Marawars, and that he would *insti-* "*gate* the great Marawar, Tondeman, and Travencore, and "other Polygars, to unite against Tanjore, and that he should "order his people from the Madura and Tinnevelly countries "to assist."—This is the constant insidious course of the Nabob with regard to all his neighbours, fomenting disputes amongst them, to end in the common destruction of them all.

It is needless to contrast this course with the conduct of the Rajah. It is perfectly known in what a moderate and equitable manner the King of Tanjore terminated these wars in which he was victorious; by receiving very moderate compensations, and by mutual marriages, according to the usages of a mild and civilized people, the object of whose wars is satisfaction and not extirmination.—Very different was the spirit of the wars afterwards carried on, by the Nabob, against both the unhappy litigant parties in this dispute; for the Nabob has actually extirminated those Polygars, and is now overwhelmed with grief, and calls on our compassion for meeting obstructions in the like pious design of destroying the King of Tanjore.

If it should be still concluded, that these Polygars, being dependents on the Nabob, could not be attacked without his leave; — to this there are very plain and conclusive answers. I have just shewn that if his leave were necessary, the King of Tanjore had his leave: but to go deeper,

* Company's Appendix, P. 652.

I must observe, first, that the Nabob must prove that the Polygars of Marawar were, or ought to be his dependents. On this point, the Presidency did think fit to institute *some* enquiry; and the result of it was, that there was *no proof of such dependency*, any farther than the transient prevalence of force, by which the powers in India have alternately robbed each other, according to the measure of their force, without any plea of right or pretence of claim. The *independent authority* of the several Polygars in their several districts, was *ancient and hereditary*, and not derived from the Nabob or any one else *. He claimed their dependency in virtue of his possession of Trichinopoly, which he usurped from an usurper, and (if it was our business to enquire into titles) holds at this hour from the rightful owner. The King of Tanjore also claimed, something like their dependence, upon probably not a much better foundation. The Presidency themselves state the matter right, when they say, "*That constitutionally they are independent of both* †." Very ready they were indeed, when weak and oppressed, to acknowledge any superior, and as willing to renounce all dependence when they were at ease and liberty, none indeed having any natural or just superiority over them. But the Nabob's paternal care and attention to these Polygars will be considered hereafter. It will then appear how much this injury to his dependents was the true cause of the war on the King of Tanjore, when I come to the proceedings of 1772;

* Company's App. P. 680, 681.

† Ibid. 682.

which

which proceedings I flatter myſelf, will appear to ſtand upon no better arguments, than thoſe which have been fully and ſatisfactorily refuted with regard to the war of 1771.

The ſucceſs of the war of 1771, as the Rajah was much weaker than the confederacy, and was taken unprovided of any alliance, was very different from what its merits deſerved. Tanjore, after the blood of its inhabitants had been freely drawn (upon the pretexts we have been juſt examining) and the country plundered, was obliged to ſubmit to a ranſom not much ſhort of £. 700,000 ſterling, and to ſuch other terms as the Nabob thought proper to exact.

SECTION V.

Breach of the firſt treaty of 1771—Pretences for that breach examined—Duplicity of the Nabob and his Party—Account of the matter as given by the Nabob's Sons and Miniſter.

THE treaty, as we have ſeen, was formally concluded: but ſuch was the condition of this unhappy country, that the duration of the treaty had no longer period, than until orders could arrive from the Nabob and the gentlemen at Madraſs, for annulling it. The author of the Conſiderations is not aſhamed publicly to ſet forth facts, which ſhew, that the Engliſh did then inſtigate the Nabob to a moſt flagrant breach

breach of the treaty, and almost instantly after its execution wrote to their general "*to that effect.*" Nothing can better explain the character of the proceedings of the Presidency than their own words, and I insert them as they are given in their own pamphlet: * "As the best means "therefore under these circumstances *to parry the mischiefs* "*of an accommodation*, they represented to the Nabob the "necessity of pursuing the line of conduct set forth in the "subsequent extracts."

"Our apprehensions arising from a peace so suddenly "concluded, and upon terms which appear to us *so insecure*, "rendered it necessary that we should take every possible "precaution, as if we were *actually on the eve of a war*; a "letter was accordingly wrote to General Smith to that "effect. *By one of the articles of the treaty, the fort of Vel-* "*lum was either to be restored to the Rajah, or to be destroyed.* "As this was a fort of the utmost importance, being in a "manner a key to Tanjore, the Nabob, *by our desire*, sent "positive orders to his Son, *on no account to deliver it up* "*without his express direction.* It was indeed the only tie we "had on the Rajah for his performance of his engage- "ments. As it would require a considerable time to demo- "lish it; if it were resolved to do so, by reason of its great "extent, we directed General Smith to leave in it a *suf-* "*ficient garrison* of the Company's troops, with a proper "quantity of stores for its defence, *and on no account to*

* Considerations, Pages 23, 24, and 25.

"*deliver*

" *deliver it up without our express orders.* In the mean time " we advised the Nabob to instruct his Son to require *punctual performance of every article of the agreement.* The Rajah had engaged to pay certain sums of money, and deliver " up certain jewels and other effects taken from the Marawar, which it is *probable he meant not to accomplish.* It " therefore seemed very justifiable, *in case of failure, to recommence hostilities*; and hostilities recommenced on such grounds " would *disannul the whole agreement*, and leave the parties at " liberty to insist on *fresh conditions* on either side. The " Nabob's Son was therefore instructed, in case this should " happen, to demand, as a *sine qua non*, the cession of the " fort of Vellum. As we *conjectured, so it proved*—The Rajah *equivocated*; our *guns had not been drawn out of the batteries*; dispositions were made for recommencing hostilities; " a fresh *negociation* ensued; the fort of Vellum, with the " districts of Coiladdy and Elangad were demanded, and " formally ceded by the Rajah." This is the account given by the parties themselves of this unparalleled breach of faith, and their motives to it.

The effect to the King of Tanjore, of the conclusion of a peace with the Nabob, was, that in that very instant he found himself " on the eve of a war with the Company." It had been agreed to restore the fort of Vellum, or to demolish it; but orders were sent, " on no account to deliver it up;" and instead of demolishing it, " it is ordered to be sufficiently " garrisoned;" and pretences are to be sought for disannulling the

the whole agreement, and enforcing fresh conditions. But the most extraordinary strain of their reasoning is this—They find the terms of the treaty inconvenient to the Nabob, and too advantageous to the King of Tanjore, and therefore they presume it "*probable* that he did not mean to accomplish "them;" and as most fortunately, every thing agreeable to their wishes turns out according to their conjectures,—" the "*Rajah equivocated,*" the treaty is gone, they open their batteries—Vellum is surrendered to them; and to make it of sufficient weight, two valuable districts are added.

The gentlemen have not been at the pains of telling us what the *equivocation* was, that proved so advantageous to them, and that fell in so aptly with their occasions and predictions. If the reader is not already nauseated with the grossness of these frauds, and the barbarity of these violences, he will think it worth his while to consider, whether they, who hoped for the annulling of a treaty in order to extract new and larger terms, were not far more likely to *equivocate*, than he whose interest it was to keep them confined to the original agreement? The reader will judge, whether those, who from the cannon's mouth had dictated a treaty in the breach of the walls of his capital, and had kept the batteries, which had reduced him to capitulate, still pointed, were not more likely to *equivocate* for their own advantage, than the unhappy besieged Prince, who could get nothing but additional oppressions by litigating or chicaning with a force, which on the instant he had found irresistible.

 It

It is not from any neceſſity of proving the futility of the pretences uſed for this breach of faith, that I proceed further in the detail of this affair. They are not even plauſible. But I dwell a little upon it, in order that from this particular affair, the reader may be furniſhed with an idea of the ſpirit of all their proceedings The Preſidency (in their Letter juſt quoted) tell us, that the King of Tanjore was obliged by the treaty to pay certain ſums of money, and to deliver up to the Nabob certain jewels taken from the Marawar, which, "it was probable, he *did not mean to accompliſh*;" and that, on the demand of them, "the Rajah *equivocated*." Unfortunately for them, in their ſtory of the equivocation, the Nabob's own Miniſter, then in the camp, Nazib Khan, tells quite another tale. He informs his maſter, that thoſe jewels (which were not worth above 3,000 pounds) were actually delivered to the Nabob's eldeſt Son, but that He, having then had his orders to break the treaty, immediately returned them. As to the money which "it was *probable* the King of Tanjore did not mean to pay;" unluckily alſo for this *probability*, the ſame Miniſter informs the Nabob, that on the day of the delivery of the jewels, the King of Tanjore had offered bills, in forty-five days, for the ſum of nine lacks, out of fourteen agreed to be paid; and it was ſettled that the remaining ſum ſhould be paid on the Monday following; and in conſequence the King of Tanjore, claimed that the batteries before the place ſhould be demoliſhed.

The fairneſs of this proceeding on the one hand, and the

ſtrict

ſtrict orders from the Nabob and the Preſidency not to fulfil the terms, threw the eldeſt Son of the Nabob, Umdut Ul Omrah, into the greateſt perplexity and diſtreſs. This virtuous Prince (whom the Durbar politics never fail to treat with diſreſpect), was not inſtantly able, even under this overbearing authority, to bring his mind to the uncoloured breach of a treaty perfectly concluded and ſettled, but a week after the ratification. Nazib Khan expreſſes the thing in a very natural manner: "He (the young Nabob) was greatly "perplexed at the peruſal of its *particular* contents, *and of* "*courſe he conſidered from morning till ten o'clock at night in order* "*to break the peace.* He likewiſe conſulted with the General "about it *."

It is no wonder that a mind not broken in by frequent acts of perfidy, ſhould ſpend a long time in ſuch a deliberation. It is probable he might have deliberated to this day, before he could find a plauſible pretext, if his younger brother, the Emir Madur Ul Mulk, a perſon of great vigour of mind and ample reſources, and one who ſupplied by natural talents his want of experience in theſe matters, had not come to his aſſiſtance. This young manly politician decided the affair by arguments altogether worthy of the occaſion. No narrative of the tranſaction can be ſo ſatisfactory as his own; it is in his letter to his Father, the Nabob: "† As the ſaid Behander" (meaning his eldeſt brother) "had *lately fixed his ſeal* to the agreement paper,

* Company's Append. P. 914. † P. 907.

"he

"he was *hesitating a little* upon it; I then told him, *He* "*must not look upon his agreement*, but that he should be al-"ways mindful to observe *your Excellency's pleasure*;" and he adds, "that if that article be not inserted in the treaty, "*it was no matter*, but now some *fresh demands* must be "specified and obtained." This, it must be confessed, was a free and easy way of proceeding. When it was objected to this worthy offspring of the Nabob, that *before the peace* every means had been used to persuade the King of Tanjore to give up the fortresses and territories, which they now resolved to force from him after the peace; the young great man, instead of looking about for pitiful excuses like his advocate, "desired him to remember the proverb, That if a "man *insists upon another man's life*, he will suffer the *pains of* "*agony* rather than part with it;" and thus he concludes the Rajah would suffer the pains of agony in quitting his territory, secured to him by the last peace, when his life was insisted on as the alternative. Accordingly he sent in fresh proposals, and threatened to renew the fire in case of non-compliance; which being told to the King of Tanjore, by *various ways and means* (I use his own expression) this unfortunate Prince was obliged to foregoe the treaty he had just made. It was in vain that the Tanjore Ambassador urged the faith of the treaty.—"* It is to be "remarked (says he) that the Tanjore Vakeel argued with "me very much at the time of our carrying our demands,

* Company's Appendix, P. 907.

"saying

"saying, that as *the treaty was already given under our seal,* it "was not proper to advance *fresh* demands." This argument did indeed seem somewhat reasonable; but the young Prince preserving exactly the same style of magnanimity to the disputing Vakeel, which he had before used to his hesitating elder brother, gave the two following answers in lieu of all reason *; and he thus describes it in his narrative to his Father: "That an order arrived from your Excellency's Court, that they *should by all means preserve your pleasure,* if not, the *war will be renewed.*" Here was no equivocation; no speculation of future breach of faith on the side of the Rajah; no talk of refusal of jewels, payments, &c.—Do this or die!—was the only argument, colour, or pretext.

The young statesman very naturally valued himself not a little on his success in this resolute measure; and to recommend his endeavours, puts his Father in mind again of the difficulties from the treaty.—"*Your* Excellency (says he), *is very sensible of the agreement made before.*" It is no wonder that his Father was so well pleased with him. He had torn away, in spite of the treaty, the fortresses of Vellum, Coiladdy, and Elangad, the keys not only of the force, but the sustenance of the King of Tanjore. That he should be bountifully rewarded was natural. But the hardship was, that the poor King of Tanjore should be obliged to reward him for this extraordinary favour. After all other payments, he

* Company's Appendix, Page 907.

made

made him a present of 12,500 pounds sterling, which I suppose, as usual, was obtained by *various ways and means.*

In this manner was broke, after a week's existence, the first treaty of 1771. A second treaty was entered into, in which, as we have seen, *the Nabob's pleasure was preserved.* They had got every thing they thought proper to ask; they had got the place which they contended for, as security, and a great deal more. The Nabob's treaty-breaking and treaty-making Son, declares it to be a "* thousand times "better than what was heretofore made." Still however, they were, it seems, as insecure as ever. The resources indeed of their insecurity, were inexhaustible. Here they had found it *probable,* that the King did not *mean* to keep the treaty which they thought proper to break in the manner we have seen. When they had found it convenient that the treaty of 1769 should be broken, they said, "That should "the King of Tanjore persist in demanding an abatement "in the Pishcush due, on account of his late charges, it "would *furnish* us with a *just pretext to accuse* him of a "breach of his engagements, and to take our measures ac-"cordingly."

The expression of "*just pretexts,*" is remarkable; these are words that have, I believe, never met together before. Justice had in fact as little connection with their actions, as the English language will suffer to exist between the words *just* and *pretexts.* Those who shew themselves so desirous of

* Company's Appendix, P. 907.

pretexts for war, and so hopeful of obtaining them, are seldom disappointed in their views; accordingly, as they found pretexts twice in 1771, it was not likely that they should be destitute of them not quite two years after, in 1773. What these *just pretexts* were, we shall see; it is the authors "grand and important period," and as such we shall treat it.

This author tell us, That at this period the gentlemen of the Presidency *, "were thrown by the Nabob's treaty with "the King of Tanjore, *into a situation of extreme delicacy*; involving at once the considerations of policy and the faith "of treaty *acceded to* by their ally."

The considerations of policy are not our present business. The embarrassment of the gentlemen arose evidently from the *faith* of the treaty, which it must be admitted is frequently very embarrassing to people's policy. Mahomet Ali had but two years before concluded a solemn treaty with the King of Tanjore; he had concluded it on just the terms he thought proper himself to dictate. This author pleases to say, that the Nabob *acceded to it*. If this were true, his accession to it bound him to observe it. The distinction, if it were founded, would do nothing in his favour; for he who accedes becomes a party from that moment, and all parties are bound.—But the fact is, he originally, as a principal, *made* the treaty, and could not accede to it, as there were no other parties to the treaty than himself and the Rajah of Tanjore. But he wished to get himself loose; and the question was, the manner

* Considerations, Page 26.

of doing it. The treaty was clear; it was recent; it was corrected, amended, and enlarged, at his own desire, and at the *instance* of the Presidency—He had acquired immense sums and important territories by it. Thus circumstanced, the violation of the treaty was really distressing to his delicacy; but the grounds of proceeding had been laid, which must prevent any difficulties that treaties could put in the way, from becoming absolutely unsurmountable.

The reader must remember the evasions which the Presidency happily invented to get rid of the treaty of 1769. *They had made* the treaty, and were bound by it; but they had the discretion to keep the Nabob *in reserve*, who (as they said) never ratified it, and he therefore was not in the same shackles. In consequence of this freedom of the Nabob, in 1771 he made war upon the Rajah; and the Company, (who did as confederates what for all the world they would not have done as principals) appeared as his allies; and their irresistible armies swept all before them. In 1773 the time was come, when the good office relative to the treaty of 1769, was to be requited to the Nabob by one of the same kind; for now the Nabob in his turn, had most unluckily got into the trammels of a treaty. The Presidency, at the time of this treaty, notwithstanding it was made according to their express directions, had cautiously, "considering themselves in the character of *Guardians* of the peace of the Carnatic, *as well* as of the *Nabob's rights*," judged it requisite to keep aloof; and as the author expresses it, "* *declined* a ratification of the

* Considerations, Page 26.

"treaty

"treaty; and to awe the Rajah into the performance of his "ſtipulations, they held themſelves in readineſs to *recommence* "*hoſtilities*, till they ſhould receive *ſolid and convincing proofs* "*of the ſincerity of his intentions*."

At this criſis, the poſition which they took was moſt extraordinary; they were neither parties to the treaty, nor ratifiers of it, nor guarantees; but they were ſtationed *to awe* the Rajah (a ſort of ſcare-crow) and to be ready to *recommence hoſtilities* in caſe he ſhould not be ſincere in thoſe engagements, in which they would have no ſhare. It is plain that there was ſomething in the written obligation of a treaty, likely to be very inconſiſtent with the part they were reſolved to act; for on any other principle it is hard to tell, why, if the convention was no convention of theirs, they were ſo engaged to keep themſelves armed to enforce it: or if, on the contrary, the object of the treaty was preſſing on them in point either of policy or juſtice, it is impoſſible to explain how they came not formally to ratify and guaranty it, as they had done the treaty of 1762, which firſt ſettled them in the character of guarantee. This character of guarantee would have given them a far more clear and equitable and ſolid right of interference, than the new character of an *armed byſtander prepared to recommence hoſtilities*, which they thought fit to create for their own uſe. But the reaſon for this conduct is plain. By having a better and more reſpectable title, they would at the ſame time have ſtood in a more limited capacity, and in a capacity too that, we see by their letter to the Directors, of 28th Feb. 1772, was the most abhorrent from the Nabob's views and wishes.—* "By that expedition, *viz.* that of 1771, he hoped "and obtained what he earnestly wished for, *viz. the re-"moval of that restraint which he thought himself under by the "Company's guarantee of* 1762." One would think that a powerful and friendly guarantee to a treaty of one's own dictating, would be a most desirable thing: yet the Nabob, who could do nothing without their forces, trembled at their guarantee; because that instrument must go to Europe, and would stand an evidence of our agreement, that must bind him and us to something or other; whereas the gentlemen at Madrass in their new capacity, and in those ample and indefinite terms of "guardians of peace," and "guardians of rights," were under no restraint whatever; and there was nothing they or the Nabob wished to do, for which they could not find abundance of *their* just pretexts.

Here then, instead of sneaking (as in the transaction of 1769) the humble retainers and followers of the Nabob, they appear in the lofty character of *guardians* of the peace of the Carnatic, as well as the *Nabob's rights.* As his guardians, they took care that the agreement concluded by their pupil himself, to the prejudice of his own rights, could not bind him (on account I suppose of his minority.) * "They "therefore" (and it is the great advantage of playing the game of fast and loose) "under this dilemma, *agreed* to an armistice;

* Company's Appendix, P. 1116. † Considerations, P. 26.

"for

" for it cannot be deemed an *abſolute termination* of the war." Certainly not; for upon their principle nothing could end that, or any war that Mahomed Ali ſhould chooſe to carry on.

It is not denied however, that it purported in terms to be an abſolute peace. Two treaties, the laſt of them made under their own directions, in a ſingle year, were not ſufficient to put an end to the war. They employ for this purpoſe a diſtinction of notable ſervice to them, though not hitherto much employed in the *corps diplomatique*. They do not *ratify*, they only *agree* to the treaty; and in their ſyſtem, a man is not to be bound to that which he agrees to. This invention, as a very ingenious refinement, will have its due praiſe; and if it be generally adopted, will free politicians from very great *embarraſſment*. They did however (they admit) in ſome way or other, *agree* to that treaty; they received ſome benefit too by the agreement; for they did, or ought to have obtained for the Company, out of the ſpoils of the Rajah, a preſent from the Nabob of ten lacks of pagodas, or £. 400,000 ſterling. The taking this money, though it was it ſeems no ratification, yet it is ſomething very like receiving the equivalent for one: yet neither the Nabob's treaty, nor their agreement, nor this beneficial effect of both, was able to form an obligation that ſhould be binding on them.

SECTION VI.

Commencement of the war of 1773—Pretexts for that war examined—Negociations with the Marattas explained—The Nabob's conqueſt of the Marawar and Nalcooty countries conſidered—The ſpirit of his government—Obſervations on the policy of conqueſt in his favour, and on the ſettlement of India.

THE Gentlemen at Madraſs having in the manner we have ſeen, ſlipped into the hands of the unfortunate King of Tanjore, an *agreement* inſtead of a *ratification*, and metamorphoſed a *treaty of peace* into an *armiſtice*; and having held themſelves ever ſince the concluſion of the treaty *in readineſs to recommence hoſtilities*, as *guardians of peace*; and, as guardians of the Nabob's rights, tolerably diſpoſed to hear his complaints, this their dutiful ward is not long before he brings before his guardians the following complaint. I ſtate it from the author. *

" By advice confirmed by Mr. Moſtyn, the Company's " reſident at Poonah, the Rajah had endeavoured to bring " the Marattas into the Carnatic."

" He not only refuſed to aſſiſt him with troops againſt the " Marawar and Nalcooty Zemindars, but he admitted them " (when defeated by the Nabob) into his own territories, and " aſſiſted theſe rebellious ſubjects with men, money, powder, " and ſhot."

* Conſiderations, P. 26 and 27.

"He had taken the runaway Polygars of Worriorpollam "and Arielore under his protection, giving them the districts "of Cumcunum for a residence."

"He has, *under the plea* of borrowing money, mortgaged "some districts of the Tanjore country to the Dutch, French, "and the Danes."

"He has refused the money agreed for by treaty, ten lacks "still remaining due."

"The select Committee took *into serious consideration* this "important representation of the Nabob; and upon *ma-* "*turely weighing* all the facts and motives with the essen- "tial interests of the Company, and the rights of their "ally, they determine not only the justice and policy, but "the necessity of reassuming vigorous measures against "the *incorrigible* Rajah; it being evident that in the *present* "*system it is dangerous to have such a power* in the heart of a "province."

"As to any rights of protection under treaties even from "1762 to the present hour, it was obvious, that he who had "violated all, had no claim to the benefits of any, especially "his gross and almost instantaneous violation of the last, in- "advertently indulged to him by the Nabob, had absolutely "forfeited every shadow of pretension; adding thereby new "demerit to his former delinquency, which has proved itself "amply sufficient to justify war."

The Presidency were in the right very *seriously* to consider and very *maturely* to weigh before they resolved that the late treaty

treaty was broken by the King of Tanjore—That he had broken all the treaties from 1762—That all his rights to protection were forfeited—That he was to be confidered as incorrigible, and—That in the prefent fyftem it was dangerous to fuffer him to exift as any power at all.

The propriety of ferioufly confidering and maturely weighing, is perfectly agreeable to their own opinion. Let us fee how much time they allowed themfelves, and what abundant materials they provided for their confideration and mature deliberation.

The Nabob's letter is dated on the 18th June 1773. Their refolution is drawn and concluded on the 22d of the fame month; that is, on the 4th day after the original complaint. In that time the whole was received, examined, and concluded. Never was a deliberation comprehending fo many objects of fact to be inquired into, and arguments to be difcuffed, difpatched in fo very fhort a time; but by this circumftance we fee the benefit of the Nabob's refidence at Madrafs (which is vaunted as one of the proofs of his good affections) by the very pleafant difpatch it gives to his affairs.

Four days was the fpace of time taken for this ferious confideration. What were the materials for it? truly neither more nor lefs than the Nabob's own charge. One would think that in a bufinefs of this fort, fome communication ought to have been made; fome anfwer ought to have been demanded; fome explanation, if not afked, ought to have been admitted. On the King of Tanjore's part it was the

rather

rather neceſſary, becauſe Tanjore had been the grand leading point of Mahomet Ali's ambition, and the firſt object of his political manœuvres, through his whole life; and therefore this great perſon was a witneſs (a little ſuſpicious) in his own cauſe. No enquiry of this kind, or of any kind, was however made, or even pretended; no colour was laid on the proceeding; no plauſible pretence was ſo much as affected; the Nabob's ſimple repreſentation was the text, and immediate war was the comment.

What theſe gentlemen refuſed to do, I will do for them, and for the reader's ſatisfaction; and in a very ſhort way examine thoſe famous grounds for war, one by one.

The firſt was Mr. Moſtyn's letter from Poonah. Before any diſcuſſion of the fact, it is impoſſible to avoid remarking on this correſpondence, that it appears rather ſingular, that the Company's ſervant, Mr. Moſtyn, ſhould not have communicated this important ſecret to the Preſidency, his maſters; and that the firſt explicit and direct account the Preſidency had of it, ſhould be through the Nabob, who is not ſaid to have ſo much as produced any letter from this his correſpondent.

Beſides, the letters not being produced, and therefore wholly failing as evidence, this ſort of correſpondence ought to have a little alarmed the Preſidency, inſtead of proving ſo ſatisfactory to them; for it ſhewed that their ſervant had his principal correſpondence with the Nabob, upon matter of infinite importance, and that his information to them was at beſt but ſecondary and ſuperficial.

As to the negotiation at Poonah:—If the writer of this piece had thought proper to reſort to his authority, the gentlemen of the Preſidency, they would have given him a full explanation of the matter, in the extract of their conſultation of the 22d June 1773. He is inexcuſable for omitting this, as he quotes ſometimes from thoſe very conſultations, leaving out however, both what goes before and what follows after the parts he uſes. Theſe omiſſions are not unimportant, as they immediately explain and elucidate the tranſaction he grounds his charge upon. They would ſhew how much evidence there was for the fact itſelf; which is only, that the intelligence communicated by the Nabob is, in *ſome meaſure* confirmed by Mr. Moſtyn; and that is all. But on a ſuppoſition of the exiſtence of ſuch endeavours on the part of the King of Tanjore, the Preſidency's own juſtification of him is as full as can poſſibly be wiſhed; nor is it neceſſary for me to prove any thing more than they themſelves confeſs: * "That the Nabob has conſtantly had "in view the deſign of conquering Tanjore, will not admit "of a doubt; and, as the honourable Court were adviſed by the Lord North, we are firmly perſuaded, that "his chief motive for concluding peace with the Rajah "at a time when our troops were upon the point of

* Company's App. Vol. I. P. 230 and 231.

"getting

" getting possession of the place, arose from his jealousy, " least the Company purposed at a convenient opportunity " to take the country from him. By that expedition " however, he obtained what he earnestly wished for, *viz.* " the removal of that restraint which he thought himself " under by the Company's guarantee of 1762. We " then expressed our firm opinion, that the peace con-" cluded without the intervention of the Company, " would not be considered by the Rajah as any security to " him; and that he would avail himself of the first oppor-" tunity of freeing himself from his apprehensions of the " Nabob. The intelligence communicated to us by the Na-" bob, of the Rajah's application to the Marattas and " Hyder Ali for assistance, is in some measure confirmed by " the advices transmitted to us by Mr. Mostyn, from Poonah. " Neither is the conduct of the Rajah in this instance to be " wondered at; the apprehensions he before had, have been " increased by the publication of the Nabob's intention of " reducing him, which has gained credit all over the coun-" try. He knows, that in our present situation we cannot " interfere in the disputes between him and the Nabob; that " *the Nabob did not even allow his Vakeel to visit the late* " *President.* Under these circumstances, it is not surprising " that the Rajah should endeavour to strengthen himself by " every means in his power, to enable him to withstand any " attempts of the Nabob against him. However, setting all

 " these

"these considerations aside, it is evident, that in the present "system, it is dangerous to have such a power in the heart "of the province: For as the honourable Court have been "repeatedly advised, that unless the Company can engage "the Rajah to their interest, by a firm promise of support in "all his just rights; we look upon it as certain, that should "any troubles arise in the Carnatic, whether from the "French or a country enemy, and present a favourable op-"portunity of freeing himself from his apprehensions of the "Nabob, he would take part against him, and at such a "time might be a dangerous enemy in the South. The "propriety and expediency therefore, of embracing the pre-"sent opportunity of reducing him entirely, before such an "event takes place, or before he has strengthened himself "by alliances with any other powers, are evident."

Here is a full justification of the King of Tanjore relative to this negotiation at Poonah, even by those who were the instruments of his ruin. It appears from this letter, that the negotiation (if it at all existed) had arisen from a just dread of the Nabob's insincerity, of his implacable enmity, and of his constancy to his prime object of making a conquest of the country of Tanjore. It appears, that the Nabob had even gone the length of cutting off all intercourse between him and the English. It appears that the danger apprehended in the *present system* was, that the present system would not secure to the King of Tanjore "all his *just* rights." How far a danger a danger of this ſort, ariſing from ſuch a ſort of cauſe, to ſuch a ſort of ſyſtem, becomes a proper ground for invading any country, and deſtroying any prince, muſt be left to thoſe who have the leaſt remains of equity, or of the common feelings of humanity, in their boſoms.

The ſecond article of the Nabob's reaſons for war, is of a kind full as extraordinary as the firſt; and ſhews how terribly this poor, innocent, ſuffering Gentleman, was puſhed to make out a charge, though no ſupport was required to it, except that of his own teſtimony. The ſecond article is—The King's having given him no aſſiſtance againſt the Polygars (or, as he calls them, Zemindars) of Marawar and Tondeman; and that after their defeat, he admitted them to a refuge in his dominions, and ſupplied them with powder and ſhot.*

The reader cannot avoid recollecting what he has read three or four pages backwards—that one of the grounds of

* "Breaking out into open hoſtility in February 1771, he invaded the territories of Marawar and Nalcooty. The Governor and Council now found "themſelves not only juſtified, but impelled to act in defence of their ally; "eſpecially as the Company determined, that their former orders to join the "Nabob againſt the Rajah, which the neceſſity of the times had obliged them "to ſuſpend, ſhould be now put in force." [a]

† "In violation of the Nabob's rights, in actual breach of his engagements "by the treaty of 1762, and in contempt of the honour and power of the "Company, who had guaranteed it;—and that as a conſummation of his perfidy, he attacked the dependents of the Nabob's government." [b]

[a] Conſiderations, P. 15. [b] Ibid. P. 17.

the

the quarrel with the Rajah, in the war of 1771, is, that the Rajah of Tanjore had made war on thoſe very Nalcooty and Marawar Zemindars,—and now his quarrel with him is, that he had *not* made war upon them. The Nabob firſt complains of the Rajah's invading them, who were, he ſays, under his protection; and now he complains of his not aſſiſting in the invaſion of the ſame perſons, as *rebels*.

The full extent of this extraordinary charge will not be evident to the reader, if he is not apprized that the indictment for theſe two contradictory offences is laid at one and the ſame time. For it was in the Nabob's invaſion of Tanjore, and as a juſtification of that invaſion in 1771, that the Rajah was charged with having made war on theſe Polygars, as dependents: and it was inſtantly after the ſubmiſſion of the Rajah of Tanjore, but about two months after this declaration, and in the very ſame year, theſe unfortunate people were invaded by the Nabob himſelf as criminals.

No one act of rebellion was alledged againſt them, *ſubſequent* to the time when he conſidered them as under his protection. It does not at all appear, that any aſſiſtance was aſked from the Rajah of Tanjore againſt them. It is improbable that any ſuch requiſition was made. It would have been at once inſolent and unneceſſary to have done ſo: Inſolent, as one of the offences alledged by the Nabob againſt thoſe people, for which they underwent a cruel puniſhment, was, that they had given no aſſiſtance to him againſt

 Tanjore;—

Tanjore;—to call on the King of Tanjore to chastize them for *that* fault, would be too much even for Mahomet Ali. It was unnecessary, because the army led by the Nabob's son to the destruction of the Polygars, had but just defeated the Rajah, and reduced him to submit to the capitulation of 1771. The Nabob never wanted any assistance against these feeble nations. The English army under his command, was infinitely more than sufficient for what it accomplished, their total destruction; and would have been more than sufficient for the ruin of twenty such. The Nabob, when he planned that war, represented it to the Company's servants at Madrass, as a matter of no sort of difficulty*. In effect it proved so at first: the taking of one of the principal places of the Marawar country, did not cost us twenty men; and the degree of length to which the war was afterwards drawn out, arose from the cruelties of the Nabob's army, and the refusal to the innocent people of those countries, of any sort of terms or security for their ancient privileges, and his depriving them of their hereditary lands which they cultivated with their manual labour. This drove many to despair, and to those extremities which result from that dreadful situation.

It is far from foreign to the purpose of this discourse, intended to shew the injustice and ill policy of making conquests for Mahometans by the British arms, to enlarge

* Company's Appendix, P. 959, 1073.

somewhat

ſomewhat on the foundation of this war, for not bearing a part in which, the kingdom of Tanjore has been ruined. The train of the Nabob's policy, and the method in which he links war into war, and conqueſt into conqueſt, is extremely curious. He firſt incites the Marawar to hoſtilities againſt the King of Tanjore; then he makes war againſt the King of Tanjore for his hoſtilities againſt the Marawar; he undertakes a third war againſt the Marawar, for not aſſiſting him againſt Tanjore; and a fourth againſt Tanjore for not aſſiſting him againſt the Marawar.

The reader recollects, that when the Marawars were, as *good ſubjects* of the Nabob, to be protected, they were in the eſtimation of thoſe, who, under that pretext, made war againſt Tanjore, *not ſubjects at all*, but independent Princes. If therefore they were not ſubjects, they could not be rebels on account of any act of hoſtility; much leſs could they be called to ſo ſevere an account as ſuch, for a neglect of any duty.

" We have ſaid more than once" (they are the members of the Preſidency themſelves, who ſpeak in their conſultations) " that we have *no abſolute proof*, that the Marawar and Nal-" cooty are tributaries and dependents on the Nabob's " government. *He aſſerts it*, and we have no proof to the " contrary." But preſently they ſolve the whole difficulty by a fair and candid explanation, which affords a key to the whole of theirs and the Nabob's politics. " Becauſe

" He"

" he" [the Nabob] " has *made them* his enemies, *therefore* it " is neceſſary that *they* ſhould be reduced. *I do not ſay it " is altogether juſt*; but JUSTICE AND GOOD POLICY ARE " NOT OFTEN RELATED." This explanation clears up every thing. But let us ſuppoſe, that the poor Polygars were obliged to aſſiſt him to any degree he pleaſed, againſt any enemy he had thought fit to provoke, it is certain, that even on that ſuppoſition, his complaint was unfounded. It is proved by the teſtimony of his own favourite Son *, that they actually did aſſiſt him, and that a large body of their troops were in our camp before Tanjore, at the time of its ſurrender: how long before does not appear; for the war was of an extremely ſhort duration. This aſſiſtance was probably given without much zeal in that quarrel. The dread of the Engliſh, I have no doubt, was the principal if not ſole cauſe of it: but if they had been the moſt cordially affected to that buſineſs, it was not in their power to have appeared in the field much before the time that we find them there. If the Nabob had thought thoſe unfortunate people deficient, He ought to have remonſtrated with them upon their conduct, and have afforded them an opportunity of juſtification or of atonement. But he had long reſolved on their entire extirpation (to uſe his own favourite term) † and therefore carefully concealed from them all his pretended grievances, and all

* Company's Appendix, P. 907. † Ibid. P. 942 and 943.

his real intentions *. These unhappy people found an English army at their doors, before they knew there was a complaint against them. The Presidency which sent it, knew that the extirpation of those Polygars (so they call the native Princes) was against the Company's orders;—yet they chose to submit an English army to the ambition of a Barbarian, and to commit the whole conduct of the war and of the peace to his discretion †; fully apprized, at the same time, of the whole extent of his destructive intentions.

The circumstances which animated them to this cruel expedition against the Marawars, ought to have touched them with compassion for the faults (had there been any such) of this miserable people. Great divisions prevailed amongst them: One part was headed "only by a poor desolate woman;" the other was a Prince in a weak and unprotected minority. These circumstances of distress, did not hinder them from proceeding to the extirpation of both Prince and People with the most unrelenting rigour. First they stormed Ramanadaporam, the capital of this *poor desolate woman* ‡. "The grenadiers and other troops employed, behaved "with remarkable steadiness and coolness during the as-"sault, and those who opposed them, died in the breach,

* Company's Appendix, P. 948. † Ibid. P. 956.

‡ The seat of a temple venerated for a peculiar sanctity all over India: it had therefore become a depository of immense riches. But the wealth was chiefly defended by this opinion of the holiness of the place, which was otherwise of little or no strength.

" with

" with great bravery. There were in the place 3,000 " fighting men, and a number of inhabitants; many of " those who carried arms were killed, some threw them- " selves over the walls, and others fled to the Ranny's " palace for protection, and there saved their lives, as the " first confusion was over before the troops advanced so " far.—The Ranny, the young Rajah, and Pitcha Pilla, the " Dewan, are prisoners: they were found with all their effects, " jewels, &c. and of course the whole of this country must, " in a few days more, fall under the Nabob's subjection.*" —Some movements of pity arose in the breasts of those who were obliged to be the actors in these tragical scenes, and the instruments of these wars, in which *policy and justice were so little related.* —" The palace (says General Joseph Smith) " is one of the best buildings I have seen in this country, " and denotes its inhabitants having lived in truly Eastern " luxury, *which I am afraid they will never experience again.* " I have seen the young Marawar, a youth about twelve " years of age; but the Ranny has been invisible, at least " to all Europeans; she has two Daughters, both fit for " matrimony. The young Nabob has taken up his quar- " ters as near them as he well can, without intruding on " their delicacy; though I believe, if their minds were " known, they wish him at a farther distance. I have felt " very much for the distresses of these miserable people,

* Company's Appendix, P. 994.

 " though

" though they drew it on themselves, by not accepting " the offers that both the Nabob and myself offered to " them †, &c."

I am almost tired of going through a narrative of the ruin of this princely family; the distribution of whose immense hereditary riches, was like to create a mutiny before their faces, while the English troops and the Nabob's were ready to draw swords on each other, for a share in their spoils. The same inhuman plundering, and the same quarrels about it, were carried on in every part of that rich country. They who would enter more into it, will find it well worthy their attention to read the whole of No. XXVI. in the Company's Papers. I cannot, however, wholly dispense with shewing something of the feelings and opinions of a brave officer, Colonel Bonjour, on that occasion; (a person who is stated by the Presidency, as having a perfect knowledge of the country, and who was certainly, on all accounts, worthy of being employed in a better service;) because they shew the condition of a country and people about to be subjected to Mahometan government.

† It no where appears what these offers were.—Whatever they might be, the not accepting the terms of an unjust invader may be accused of imprudence, but nothing else. The fact appears by a letter of Colonel Bonjour's (p. 1000.) that she would be ready to submit to any terms, except giving up the Fort; which she calls her house, and is resolved to defend to the last extremity. By the letter too from Calecoil it appears, that the Nabob wished to have the places taken by force, and to make no peace.

It was written after the Company's troops had reduced most if not all the strong places in the Marawar country.—" * It is necessary to acquaint you" [the Presidency] " with circumstances that came lately to my " certain knowledge; by which you will perceive, that " all the plan I recommended in my Letter to the " Nabob, Waulau Jan, which Letter *you declined delivering* " *to him*, would not answer the purpose of absolutely " settling this country, *if the basis of the former govern-* " *ment is not restored to its original position.* This former " government you must, in some measure, consider the same " as those formerly established in Europe, under the denomi- " nation of Feudal Government; by which men had land " allowed to them by the Lords, which land they cultivated, " or had the inspection of, and the produce became their " property, in consequence of being engaged to take arms " at any time the country was exposed, or the Lords had " occasion for their services. *This government seems to have* " *been established from great antiquity in the Marawars*; which " country being formerly united under a Rajah, did produce " an army of fifty or sixty thousand men for its defence: " but since its division into two provinces, its force fell in " proportion to the disunion of the heads; who, *when we* " *undertook the conquest*, were not only in discord, but also " the people disaffected by reasons not material to report.

* Company's Appendix, P. 1057.

" *Expecting*

" *Expecting a continuation of their ancient privileges, they re-*
" *mained at their ploughs, and in ſome meaſure facilitated the*
" *means of conquering their Chiefs.* Since the reduction of
" the different forts in theſe countries, the people (except a
" few vagabonds) have remained *in a peaceable manner, till*
" *the Nabob determined to take from them thoſe lands which*
" *they expected to retain*; ſo that at preſent the ploughmen,
" aggravated by the loſs of their lands, have taken arms
" all over the country, and even in their own villages
" form parties of obſervation againſt ours. In this ſituation
" ſituation I muſt repreſent to you, that the ſettling this
" country in *the manner expected by the Nabob, requires ex-*
" *tremities of a ſhocking nature*; and after all, it is not to be
" ſaid that matters will be adjuſted ſo as to anſwer the ſa-
" tisfaction of all parties. Thoſe people, being both ſoldiers
" and ploughmen, have the advantage of appearing in what
" ſhape they pleaſe before our troops, and never expoſe them-
" ſelves without being ſure of the advantage. When we
" are marching we find, all over the country, moſt villages
" abandoned by the men, *there remaining in them only women*
" *and children, whom it is likely, if the Nabob perſiſts in this un-*
" *dertaking, muſt, with other poor innocents, become a ſacrifice to*
" *this conqueſt.* For if any of our baggage remains behind,
" it is uſually taken, our parties and ſtragglers are attacked:
" this is done by the inhabitants of ſome village or other.
" Theſe villages being pointed out to me, I cannot paſs the

"outrage without punishment; and not finding the objects "upon which my vengeance should fall, I can only deter-"mine it by reprisals, which will oblige me *to plunder and "burn those villages; kill every man in them; take prisoners the "women and children. These are actions which the nature of "this war will require*; for having no enemy to encounter, it "is only by severe examples of that kind, that we may expect "to terminate it so as to answer the end proposed. *I wish "his Excellency the Nabob had well balanced the advantages he "may gain, with the risk we run, in this undertaking, before he "determined to take from those people the lands in question.* "They are, besides, not so despicable as not to deserve the "privilege of keeping the mentioned land for their occa-"sional services, if regulated so as to oblige every one to be "provided with a pike of a fixed dimension, when called to "the field; and intermixed with a few Seapoys, they would be "very formidable to black cavalry, &c. being such as to en-"dure great fatigues, and to require but little wants. The "above, Honourable Sir and Sirs, will sufficiently represent "to you my sentiments in regard of settling this country, "without entering into further details: I have communi-"cated the same to the Nabob Umdut Ul Omrah, Behander, "who seems to agree with my opinion, but I do not know "what resolution will be taken.—*Wishing to see your arms "employed for a wise and more glorious purpose, than the one in "agitation*, I have the honour to remain, &c."

Such

Such was the original juſtice of the war againſt this unhappy country; ſuch the mode of carrying it on; ſuch the fruits of the conqueſt; and ſuch the ſpirit of the Nabob's Government, wherever we make conqueſts for him. Here too we ſee that the Preſidency did not dare or chuſe to make remonſtrances to the Nabob, on the abuſe of advantages obtained by our own arms. After this, it will not, I ſuppoſe, be thought a great crime in the King of Tanjore (to whoſe not leſs miſerable caſe I return) if he did not ſhew great alacrity in this moſt unjuſtifiable war.

After the defeat of the Polygars (it ſeems) the Rajah admitted them into his own territories, and ſupplied them with powder and ſhot. No proof is given nor aſked of this fact; and it is neither true nor probable as it ſtands in the charge. " He (the King of Tanjore) not only " refuſed to aſſiſt him with troops againſt the Marawar " and Nalcooty Zemindars, but he admitted them (when " defeated by the Nabob) into his own territories, and " aſſiſted theſe rebellious ſubjects with men, money, powder, " and ſhot."

It does not appear that the Nabob thought of making this complaint whilſt the grievance was freſh, and the matter, if true, was evident: it required two years to aſcertain it. One of theſe Polygar's, then very young, had been cruelly butchered by the Nabob's troops at the taking of one of his

* Conſiderations, Pages 27.

places: Him the King of Tanjore could neither receive nor assist. The poor desolate woman, who had been robbed in the sanctuary of her temple, never after was in a condition to carry on any war—These hostilities therefore, stand on the word of the accuser. As to the supposed reception of the Polygars into his territories—If he did give to these unfortunate gentlemen. of his own cast and kindred, some charitable relief in their distress, it does not seem a cause, scarcely a *pretext*, for the English to subvert the Kingdom of Tanjore. It is the same thing however to the Presidency, whether the charges on him or on the Polygars, were well or ill grounded. They never enquired into them; they took the whole on the Nabob's bare narration, and executed his orders as if they had been his Divan, and not the Council of the East India Company, and the English Nation.

The third charge is a parcel of the second; that is, that "* he had taken the *runaway* Polygars of Worriarpollam and "Allianore under his protection, giving them the districts of "Conconum for a residence."

A fine ground of war! The Nabob calls a man a *Runaway*; and then if any *neighbour* is humane enough to receive him, that act becomes an offence of such a magnitude, that the offender is to be destroyed by the English arms.—But when was this offence laid? Had the King notice to refuse the admission of these Runaways into his country, or notice to dismiss them?

* Considerations, P. 27.

Not one word. When did the gentlemen concerned in this affair, examine in what this offence of *running away* consisted, which made an act of humanity to the offenders so heinous a crime? A crime of such a dye, as to be punished by the pillage, imprisonment, and deposition of a great prince? But what ends all defence for such acts, is this, that no proof was before the Council of Madrass, that the Rajah of Tanjore was at all guilty of this act of humanity. In their eyes it may, I allow, have been a great crime. But how came they to proceed to the punishment of that crime, without any trial? The mention of the Polygars of Worriarpollam and Allianore, only serves to call up in our memory the other unjust and inhuman proceedings, by which these Princes were deprived of their patrimony, and made a sacrifice to the tyranny of the Nabob. It may make a part in the enquiry, when an account is called for, of the almost uninterrupted chain of robberies carried on for near twenty years in that harrassed country.

The fourth charge rises upon the others—" The Rajah had, " under the plea of borrowing money, mortgaged some " districts of the Tanjore country to the Dutch, French, and " Danes." The matter of this charge happens to be in some part a matter of fact; in others, as usual, it is totally unfounded.

The King of Tanjore was obliged, on the *plea* of borrowing, as his enemy stiles it, *actually* to borrow of the Dutch, in in 1771, in order to enable him to resist the Nabob's treacherous invasion; and to mortgage to them, that is, to the Dutch (and not to the French) some of his most valuable jewels, and some part of his territories. This *fact*, which the Nabob has the confidence to call only a *plea*, is confessed, and even insisted upon by himself. For, in his late memorial, * he takes credit for having redeemed these very jewels, and those very territories, by the payment of large sums; and he charges this payment on the revenues of Tanjore, after they had been rescued out of his hands. The matter between the parties in short, stands thus: He forces the Rajah of Tanjore, by invasion and violent extortions, to mortgage some of his territories, and then he makes that mortgage a reason for robbing him of all the remainder.

The fifth and last charge:—† "He refused the money "agreed for by treaty, 10 lacks still remaining due."—If this were true, it should naturally have engaged the Presidency to enquire, whether the non-payment amounted (as the charge had stated) to a refusal, or only to a delay; and whether a man, whose powers had sunk under such immeasurable extortions, was not an object meriting some support, rather than further, and even the utmost depression. The matter of the charge immediately preceding, that is, his mortgage to the Dutch, if it proved delinquency, indicated

* Company's Appendix, P. 1541.
† Considerations, P. 27.

at

at the ſame time a very great appearance of diſtreſs; ſince the unfortunate object of it was obliged, in ſuch a manner, to diſmember his territories, and to mortgage them, wherever uſury was left free to aid againſt extortion. Theſe gentlemen were, however, perfectly uniform in their conduct. The truth and the criminality of the fact, as in all their other caſes, were to be admitted by them without the leaſt degree or pretence of enquiry whatſoever. With them, the wealth and the poverty of the King of Tanjore were to be equally his crimes. What muſt be the reader's ſurprize (who may be unacquainted with their tranſactions, and the boldneſs of their advocates) to find that this money, which was ſaid by the Nabob, and admitted by the Council of Madraſs, and here repeated by their advocate, to have been *refuſed*, was, at the time of making the accuſation, actually *paid!*

The King of Tanjore knowing (though, indeed, knowing but in part) with what cruel and rapacious enemies he had to deal, moved heaven and earth to raiſe money for the ultimate payment. Having exhauſted the foreign ſettlements, he applies himſelf to an active money dealer, one Comora, an Hindoo of his own religion, adjuring him, by every tye that they held dear in common, not to ſuffer a Prince and People of his own perſuaſion, to become a ſacrifice to the Mahometans. He deſires bills upon Madraſs to the amount of the laſt payments, and pledges a territorial revenue for the ſecurity.

6 This

This Comora was the Dubash or Agent of the famous Mr. Paul Benfield, the Nabob's banker. Whether moved by sentiments of conscience, as he pretended, or thinking the money of his master to be well vested in the territory to be engaged for it, and in an hurry to receive the usury for a payment that was to be made to themselves; or having planned from the beginning, the villany that was afterwards executed, he drew bills on his master, Mr. Paul Benfield, for the money; which bills were put into the Nabob's hands. The deluded King of Tanjore thinking he had at length set himself on secure ground, wrote to the Presidency, that as he had punctually discharged the last payment, he now hoped that he had entitled himself to the Nabob's friendship. But he was mistaken—the Nabob's friendship was too valuable a thing to be so slightly purchased. With these bills in his hands, or in his banker's hands (a fact that has since been confessed by Mr. Benfield himself) he was not ashamed to make the above charge of a refusal of payment; and sent the English troops to invade and conquer that very kingdom, for the exorbitant ransom of which he had just received the last payment.

On these pleas of the Nabob, the Presidency, as if they had a grave and plausible matter before them, finally sit in judgment,—but not with both the parties before them. They declare all ideas of the existence of a guarantee of the King of Tanjore, on the part of the Company, removed; and without a pretence of their being guarantees of any treaty on the part of the Nabob, they take into

consideration

consideration "The propriety and necessity of the expedi-
"tion against Tanjore;" and they assign the three following most curious reasons for engaging in it. 1st. "That in con-
"sequence of the *humiliating condition* to which the Rajah
"has been *obliged to submit at the conclusion of the last peace,*
"*and his constant apprehensions of the Nabob's taking possession of*
"*his country*, he *must* be willing to join the French, or any
"power." 2dly. "Because his total reduction becomes matter
"of *self-defence*." 3dly "Because the Nabob will pay his debts
"in case of disturbances, which he declares he never will do
"if they will not undertake this expedition *."

They who will take the trouble of comparing these raw, uncoloured pretexts, with those of the same kind made on a former occasion, with regard to the King of Tanjore (which I have stated in a note, (page 49.) and with regard to the Marawar Princes (recited in pages 96, 97.) will find a great uniformity in their whole system. First it is their practice to do the greatest injuries to the native sovereigns; they reduce them to the *most humiliating condition*; they fill them with fear and *apprehensions of taking possession of their country*; and then, kindly to free them from all causes of dread, they realize the evils which they had made them apprehend; they fall upon them; they plunder and subdue them. They conclude from their treatment of them, that the Princes *must* be their enemies, and then their *total reduction* becomes matter of

* Company's Appendix, P. 1129.

self

ſelf defence. To crown the whole; becauſe their Mahometan friend and patron refuſes to pay his debts, without a pretence of quarrel, they join him to exterminate their neighbours, benefactors, friends, and allies.

Theſe are the grounds and principles (I ſhall beſtow no epithets upon them) upon which the Nabob proceeded, in the year 1773, with Engliſh arms, to the ruin of Tanjore. In this invaſion, as much blood was ſhed as the reſiſtance could admit. Then, with a relentleſs hand, he proceeded to pillage the country to the amount, including the perception of the revenues, of more than four millions ſterling.

This the conſiderer and his party, call "*juſtice and policy,* "*and the neceſſity of reaſſuming vigorous meaſures againſt the in*"*corrigible Rajah. It being evident, that in the preſent ſyſtem* "*it was dangerous to have ſuch a power in the heart of the* "*province.*"

For the purpoſe of annihilating *ſuch a power in their preſent ſyſtem,* they invented a conſtruction for public engagements, in virtue of which they annulled the treaty of 1762 by that of 1769. By this conſtruction they annulled the treaty of 1769 by the firſt treaty of 1771, and the firſt treaty that year they annulled by the ſecond; and then they annulled both the treaties of 1771, by the invaſion and uſurpation of 1773. The author, who does not like that this curious treaty-breaking invention ſhould be diſcredited, complains of having the exiſtence of the fundamental treaty of

1762

1762 ſtill ſuppoſed. He is abſolutely outrageous againſt the Directors for ſo conſidering it. * "We trace," ſays he, "an "ignorance and negligence, which though it exculpates them "in ſome meaſure from intentional miſchief, was cer-"tainly very criminal in matters of ſuch high concern." The gentleman's zeal and warmth againſt theſe high crimes and miſdemeanors of the Company againſt its ſervants, will not permit him to recollect, that the Direction had never ratified any treaty, but that of 1762; and that their whole correſpondence goes upon an idea of its exiſtence, as a baſis of their right of interference in the diſputes between the Nabob and the Rajah. He forgets that the gentlemen concerned in the war of 1771, ſuppoſe its exiſtence (at leaſt at that time) ſince they declare that they acted *partly* as its guarantees. He forgets alſo that the Directors, under all the deceptions proved to be practiſed upon them, never authorized any treaty, or any war, but for the ſuppoſed purpoſe of enforcing that original fundamental treaty.

As to the conqueſt; the directors conſidered it, as what it was, a ſhocking uſurpation. If we have proved that the Nabob was the aggreſſor and wrong-doer, by the author's rule, he ought to have no benefit of treaties, and ſuch a power ought not to exiſt: But I do not wiſh that his own principles ſhould be brought home to the Nabob; I do not wiſh that any reigning power ſhould be *extirpated*, though every honeſt man

* Conſiderations, P. 40.

muſt

muſt wiſh, that they ſhould all of them be kept within the bounds of juſtice; and that we, as an example of the leſſon we teach to others, ſhould keep ourſelves within the ſame limits. This is what every Engliſhman has a right to demand.

On this ſtate of the grounds and principles of the conqueſt of Tanjore (not aſſumed but proved) the public will judge of the propriety of the Company's meaſures, for reſtoring it to the natural ſovereign and its original government, and of the wildneſs of the ſtring of ſchemes, propoſed in the pamphlet I am examining, for tearing it again from thoſe natural holds, and once more ſubjecting this harraſſed country to the ferocious rapacity of Mahometan deſpotiſm.

If Mahomet Ali had originally no right, or colour of right, to have Tanjore conquered for him by Engliſh arms, he has no right to have it returned to him by a third violence on the people, and a ſecond depoſition of the unhappy King of that country, who neither has furniſhed, nor in his preſent ſtate can furniſh, any kind of pretence for ſuch an outrage. His country is poſſeſſed by Engliſh troops; to this he has moſt chearfully conſented: he paid, in little more than a year after his reſtoration, and out of a country ruined by the ravages and extortions of the Nabob, £. 320,000 ſterling, for the protection of the Company. He has ſince granted of his free bounty, Nagore, a territory of value, both for ſituation and profit, to the Company.—Yet after all, he is not

 now

now at eafe from their fervants, who have not yet ceafed to give countenance to the Nabob's claim of debt; and who even canvafs and litigate the value of his late gift, as if it was a debt to themfelves. Can that country be fubject at once to the Englifh and to the Mahometans? Can the King pay all their multiplied demands? and after having yielded himfelf and his country to the Company at their own requeft, on their own terms, and on their own faith, is he to be delivered over to Mahomet Ali, his bigotted as well as his political enemy?

If this idea be not fupportable, it is unneceffary for me to take notice of the feveral ingenious modes and conditions of executing the project for a furrender of Tanjore to the Nabob, which is elaborately argued in the latter end of the pamphlet before us *. I fhall only touch upon fome of the extraordinary fcattered topics of the author. This gentleman feems to think, that the King of Tanjore is fo near being a prifoner to the Englifh, with their garrifon in his fort, that he will not be much worfe off by being totally depofed and made a prifoner to the Nabob. Pray, good Sir, let him judge for himfelf. It is not the Nabob and his partizans, that the King of Tanjore wifhes to make his referrees. It is very true, that it is not what is beft, but what is not worft of all, that is now in the King of Tanjore's option. If the King of Tanjore muft be a prifoner, he does not choofe to be prifoner to the Nabob. He is ready to depend on the benevolence of a

* Confiderations, p. 68.

British King, and a British corporation created and acting by law; though he cannot rely on the mercy of Mahómet Ali, and his Durbar.

But our author tells us, that the Nabob when he has deposed the King of Tanjore, will give him security for a pension on his revenues. To this excess of Mahomet's generosity, the King of Tanjore will answer, that he chooses to take his own income himself out of his own territories. Limited as his revenue is, it is still a better security for some kind of rank and authority, than Mahometan faith for a miserable pension.

The Nabob's own, his eldest, Son, starves on his Father's pension; though a Jaghire land is assigned for the payment of it. The Rajah would something doubt of better treatment than this "* good old Prince" (in our author's language) chooses to give his own child. The King of Tanjore too, remembers well the Nabob's generosity, in the jewels that were torn from the ears of his women; he remembers his own poor and miserable prison; he remembers the credit which the Nabob has since assumed for not having actually taken away his life; he remembers the bare walls to which he was restored, of what had been one of the richest palaces in the world; he remembers, that he owed to private benevolence, that he had a carpet to sit on, or a palankeen to carry him. On the whole, therefore, the Rajah prefers

* Considerations, Pages 57.

the worst treatment that the worst humours of the Company's servants can mortify him with, to the tender mercies of a Mahometan master, however the partizans of Mahomet Ali may applaud and magnify the benevolence of his nature.

The author ridicules the idea of the King of Tanjore being in reality restored, whilst English garrisons possess his forts; yet he is not ashamed to propose this very same thing on the delivery of the country to the Nabob (whom he is pleased to consider as the lawful owner.) He proposes the very same arrangements * as to the garrison of the places by English; but he proposes it with great caution; for he knows that the Nabob having once had English garrisons in all his fortresses, found means to remove them all, and to form a great standing army of his own, trained in the European manner, in the hopes of supporting his new scheme of independence, recommended to him by English friends and partizans.

This gentleman, (the author of the Considerations) and all those who engage in the cause of Mahomet Ali, in proposing schemes of government, and supporting rights of government in the East, are pleased to confine their attention solely to Princes, and to the rights of Princes. The wretched *people* are no part whatsoever of their consideration. Every man who knows any thing of India, must know the utter

* Considerations, P. 69. " Be it agreed, *for the general safety, that the Company shall garrison the principal forts in Tanjore*, and keep up such a force as " the Nabob may deem competent to the defence of that kingdom."

3 detestation

deteſtation thoſe people entertain (I think with very good reaſon) but whether with good reaſon or not, they do moſt certainly entertain, of Mahometan government. To ſay nothing of the genius of that government in general, and in particular of the government of Mahomet Ali, it will be hardly believed, that all men do not infinitely prefer a ſubjection to Princes of their own blood, manners, and religion; that they will not be more obedient to ſuch Princes; and that ſuch Princes will not be reciprocally more tender of them. This natural and reciprocal partiality, is matter of great conſideration in all governments; but it is peculiarly ſo among thoſe nations where there is no ſettled law or conſtitution, either to fix allegiance, or to reſtrain power.

If the Company, who under the name of alliance, or under even the name of ſubjection to a Mogul, are in reality now the actual Sovereigns and Lords paramount of India, ſtill chooſe, as hitherto they have done, and as in wiſdom perhaps they ought to do, to have a dependent government interpoſed between them and the native people, it is both their intereſt and duty that it ſhould be ſuch as is congenial to the native inhabitants, correſpondent to their manners, and ſoothing to their prejudices. The native Indians, under their own native government, are, to ſpeak without prejudice, a far better people than the Mahometans; or than thoſe who by living under Mahometans, became the depreſſed ſubjects, or the corrupted inſtruments of their tyranny; they are of far milder

milder manners, more induſtrious, more tractable, and leſs enterpriſing.

The Arabians, and Tartars, and Perſians, and their Clans of Muſſulmen, are full as rapacious, and infinitely more fierce and cruel, than the Engliſh who are ſent to make their fortunes in India in a civil or military capacity. The Engliſh have neither the ſame diſpoſition, nor the ſame degree of boldneſs, nor in many caſes, even the ſame means of oppreſſion. Without however diſputing which is the more intolerable weight, it is certain, that the people cannot bear two ſuch riders. It was our buſineſs to reſpect *poſſeſſion* as the only title that can be valid, where a great empire is broken up; and the rather, as it is the title on which we ourſelves ſtand. It was our buſineſs, that no antiquated claims ſhould be revived; and no diſturbances raiſed on ſuch dangerous pretences. It was our duty, in order to make ſome ſort of compenſation for the miſchiefs inſeperable from a foreign and commercial ſuperiority, to keep a ballance of juſtice and proportion in the ſeveral powers that were ſubordinate to us; and the laſt thing in the world which we were juſtified in doing, was to encourage arbitrary and boundleſs pecuniary demands, under the barbarous names of Nazirs, Crores, &c. &c. and leaſt of all ought we to ſupport ſuch demands in favour of any perſon whoſe own ſtrength was not ſufficient to enforce his own injuſtice. When we did this, then it became not the robbery of another, but our own. Extortion, always the endemial diſtemper

diſtemper of that part of the world, began to be aggravated in all its ſymptoms, when Aſiatic avarice was ſupported by European arts and diſcipline. Whereas our evident duty, and our cleareſt intereſt, was to employ thoſe arts and that diſcipline, and the power that grew out of them, to meliorate the condition of the ſubject and the dependent, rather than to enforce the wild claims of a pretender, or to enforce the intolerable deſpotiſm even of the lawful poſſeſſors of power. All this we might have done, and in a great meaſure may ſtill do, without any ſort of diminution (to ſpeak within compaſs) of revenue; and with an infinite increaſe of our reputation. But fatally, we have ſuffered, for a long time, a contrary courſe to prevail, to the ruin of the fine country that has fallen into our hands; and England has thought proper to look on unconcerned, whilſt the Engliſh arms have been employed by a ferocious and inſatiable Mahometan, to exterminate near twenty native hereditary princes, of very ancient, and in that part of the world, illuſtrious families. But though this depredation and ruin, and in many inſtances this total extinction, of noble houſes, be itſelf a matter which commonly excites no ſmall degree of commiſeration in all liberal minds; yet it is a conſideration infinitely inferior to that of ſuch multitudes of the native people, once under the dominion of theſe depoſed Princes, but who are now ſubjected to the intolerable burden of the Mahometan yoke. The poverty and depopulation of the country which has

enſued,

ensued, is a thing to be deplored; and surely the cause of such serious evils ought to be speedily investigated.

If there was a real disposition to investigate, and to redress these grievances, it would not be a matter of difficulty to lay before the public, in clear and distinct particulars, the horrors of the Mahometan government in India, as it is exercised in its most destructive manner by the Nabob of Arcot, as well in those territories of which the English arms had originally put him in possession, as in those of which they have made him master, by a series of near twenty years violence, war, and desolation: but as that great and necessary work is not yet undertaken, it will be sufficient, for the present, to lay before the reader some hints of what appeared to the Company at several periods, to be the spirit of Mahometan domination; its tendency to destroy the eminent nobility, who were compelled by us to a dependence upon it; and some small part of its oppressive consequences on the low and industrious part of the Indian community. It must be allowed, to the Company's honour, that they have in general endeavoured to check these excesses, though with little effect, as we have seen. However, their views seem to be perfectly conformable to the opinions of the best judges of the state of affairs in India *, and to the plan of

* "You will see," says Colonel Bonjour, "by my Letter to his Highness the Nabob, *that force of arms alone will not effect the settling and tranquility of this country*. This, I must enforce, by requesting you will support my opinion before him; for *I cannot promise you any thing favourable from the* "*operations*

of government here laid down. "We apprehended," say they in their letter to the President and Council at Fort Saint George, dated 4th March 1767, "that if any thing "can give us the interior, peaceable, and quiet possession of "the Circars*, it will be such a kind of government as "shall make the several Rajahs and Zemindars feel and "acknowledge its justice, mildness, and equity, above all "others that they have been accustomed to; so long as "they live in obedience and fulfil the engagements they "are bound to: effects which we much doubt whether "they would ever have derived *from* the Company's go-"vernment, had the *Nabob, or any other native of Indostan,* "*been entrusted with the particular management.* What we "have said, implies a confidence in *you*, that the Rajahs, "Zemindars, and every other inhabitant, will be protected "in the possession of their *just and hereditary rights:* we "mean not only as relative to oppression from the mem-"bers or ministers of *our own government*, but also from the "encroachments and attempts of each other †." — They think a *ballance of power* ought to be kept between them; that therefore "they wish the present Indian powers to

"*operations I may direct, when they are not supported by a system of government* "*suitable to the genius, customs, and privileges of the people who are to be influenced* "*by it.*" Letter from Colonel Banjour to the Presidency of Madrass. Company's Appendix, P. 1046. This letter the Presidency did not choose to deliver to the Nabob.

* The territories in the Kingdom of Goconda, acquired by the Company within a few years.

† Company's Appendix, Page 511.

" *remain* as a check upon one another *."—" That they " mean to diſtribute to every man his own; and by a " juſt, mild, and prudent conduct towards them, to evince, " that conqueſts and plunder are not the objects of our " purſuits †."—They forbid " the extirpation of the Poly- " gars §, though they wiſh them in obedience to the " Nabob."—" They obſerve with concern, that in certain " countries ‡, their troops have been put to *diſagreeable* " *ſervices*, more eſpecially as the rebellion of the Polygars " may, they fear with *too much juſtice*, be aſſigned to the " *mal-adminiſtration of the Nabob's collectors*."—" That it was " repugnant to humanity, to force them to ſuch *dreadful* " *extremities as they underwent*."—" That *ſome* examples of ſe- " verity *might* be neceſſary, but it ſhould be on the *leaders* " when they fall into the Nabob's hands, and *not by the* " *deſtruction of the country*."—" That the falſe policy of " this ſhould be repreſented to the Nabob, &c."—" ‖ That " they fear his government is by no means of the mildeſt; " and that there is great oppreſſion in collecting his re- " venues **."

The Company who knew, and therefore wiſhed to diſ-countenance, his oppreſſions of the native princes and no-bility and of the people at large, in the collection of the re-venues, were alſo perfectly apprized of his peculiar oppreſſions

* Company's Appendix, P. 519.

† Ibid. P. 523.

‡ Thoſe reduced by us to a ſubjection to Mahomet Ali.

§ Madura and Tinnevelly.

‖ Company's Append. P. 523.

** Ibid. 524.

on

on the ſources of all revenue, the manufacturers of the country. Theſe manufacturers they knew were obliged to fly into the ſtrong holds of the Indian Princes, for a protection againſt Mahometan tyranny; which is a practical proof worth an hundred arguments, to decide the difference between the two governments. The Company therefore direct, " That in reducing the Polygars, they were to be " cautious not to deprive the *weavers* and manufacturers " of the protection they often meet with in the ſtrong " holds of the Polygar countries."*—And in their Letter " to the Nabob himſelf, they think fit (knowing his practice) to give him the like caution: " We entreat your Excellency " in particular, to make the *manufacturers* the objects of " your tendereſt care; particularly, that *when you root out* " *the Polygars*, you do not deprive the *weavers of the pro-* " *tection they enjoyed under them*†."

It is unneceſſary to obſerve to the reader, that when the Company permitted the Nabob to deſtroy the protection which the manufacturers enjoyed againſt his tyranny, their humane advice to him, with relation to thoſe miſerable wretches, when he had got them once more into his power, was likely to be but of ſmall benefit or conſolation to them. I have therefore quoted this paſſage, not to ſhew the efficacy of the Company's interference with their *counſels*, againſt the effects of their *arms*, but to ſhew their ſtrong ſenſe of the probable condition of thoſe whom they were going to

* Company's Appendix, p. 524. † Ibid. p. 527.

ſurrender to the Nabob's mercy: It is not wholly unlike the kindneſs of the Liſbon Inquiſition, when they deliver a miſerable Jew to the ſecular arm. Even the Preſidency of Madraſs, which at the very time it was preparing to make the war of 1771 againſt the King of Tanjore, in order to extend the ſphere of the Nabob's tyranny, ſpeaking of the diſtreſſes which a country, already ſubjugated to him, had ſuffered from a moſt grievous and waſteful war (brought on ſolely by his reſtleſs ambition) expreſs themſelves of his government in the following manner: "That they" [the diſtreſſes by the war] "have been certainly *great*; but thoſe "by the *Nabob's oppreſſions* we believe *to be greater than all*, "becauſe *they are without intermiſſion*; the other are *temporary*; "by all which oppreſſions, we believe, the Nabob has great "wealth in ſtore."

It would be perfectly uſeleſs to remark on theſe diſpoſitions and proceedings of the Nabob, if the cauſe of the evil and the means of redreſs were not both in ourſelves. All this ambition, pride, and tyranny of Mahomet Ali, and all the uſurpations and oppreſſions by which this enormous wealth have been hoarded by him, are wholly ſupported by an unnatural and extrinſic force. The Engliſh commanders, who had the misfortune to have ſome of the Nabob's troops as an incumbrance on their operations in his favour, declare, "that they could have no dependence on them," and that "they were the worſt they had ever ſeen *." The Company

* Company's Appendix, P. 1165.

 has

has frequently expreſſed the ſame ſentiments, and given their directions accordingly.—" That the Nabob is univerſally " known to be a man of no reſources in himſelf."—" A " Nabob who cannot ſupport himſelf."—" That his army " is an uſeleſs rabble."—" That the leaving the fortreſſes " of the Carnatic to his defence, would be to expoſe the " very being of the Company on the coaſt of Coromandel, " to the greateſt riſk *." On that account, they heavily and juſtly accuſe their ſervants for engaging to effectuate ſo deſperate a deſign. " On tracing the ſubject minutely, we " find, that no ſooner was the Nabob put in poſſeſſion of the " ſaid forts, and the Company's troops removed, than his " own rebellious ſubjects were hardy enough to attempt " † *re-taking* ſome of them; and their ſucceſs ſhews, that " they *had little more to do than to appear before them, in* " *order to obtain poſſeſſion.* On which account the Nabob " himſelf declared, *he was tired out with the frequent accounts* " *received of the depredations of the plunderers,* and that he " was fully convinced *his troops* were utterly unequal to " the taſk of ſuppreſſing them. ‡"

This Potentate, ſo deſcribed by the Company, and ſo deſcribed by himſelf,—a Potentate, who is ſo far from being in a condition to defend himſelf againſt a foreign enemy §, that

* Company's Appendix, P. 538.

† *N. B.* The word *re-taking* is remarkable; for, in fact, he has but few places which have not, at ſome time or other, been violently taken by the Company's Servants from the lawful Proprietors, and delivered to him.

‡ Company's Appendix, P. 541.

§ The Marattas claim, and at times exact a chout or tribute from him.

he

he is not able to ſupport the police in his own territories without an Engliſh army—has had theſe important fortreſſes, contrary to repeated orders from Europe, delivered up to his garriſons; has had conqueſts of vaſt territories made for him by our blood and treaſure, againſt the ſame repeated orders, and millions of unhappy people, without check or control of any kind, delivered over to his arbitrary diſcretion. This Potentate on ſufferance, this creature of natural and indefeaſable dependence, whoſe very power exiſts in his ſubjection, is ſet up, not only as an independent Sovereign, but as a great Conqueror. The very perſons, without whom he has no exiſtence, have thought proper, in ſpite of his unalterable imbecility, to declare themſelves his vaſſals, and to act ſo much in that character, "that," as they themſelves tell us, "the "*Engliſh* are conſidered in India as indeed *great and* "*powerful*, but that they are *entirely ſubordinate to the* "*Nabob, and obliged to employ that force according to his* "*pleaſure*." He who is himſelf abroad a bugbear, and at home a ſhadow, is however, by the juſt terrors of our ſubſtantial power, become dreadful to almoſt all his neighbours; and within his own territories exerciſes an oppreſſion, which outrages humanity, over the Princes and people, not yet extirpated, whom we have bowed to his yoke, but which the weakneſs and deſpotiſm of his government would have both provoked and enabled them effectually to ſhake off, if the dread of the immediate march of the army of a Chriſtian and free people to ſuccour Mahometan deſpotiſm, did not even forbid them ſo much as to complain under their ſufferings.

Formerly the Vakeels or Agents of the Indian Princes, were admitted to Madraſs; their complaints were heard, and their claims were conſidered. If juſtice was not always done, it was never formally denied; and the Engliſh Company appeared as a power of dignity in India. But at preſent, they are taught to direct their eyes to the Nabob as principal.—Of late, almoſt every agent from every ſtate in India, has been excluded from the leaſt correſpondence with our Preſidency; whilſt the Durbar of the Nabob was ſurrounded with ſuch a crowd of foreign miniſters, as gave it the air of an imperial court. * They ſubmitted (or as they ſay, were compelled to ſubmit) to this humiliation, and conſented to exiſt for no other purpoſe than as Agas of the Janizaries, to the Durbar of Mahomet Ali. Whenever he wants to make a conqueſt, or to ſuppreſs any rebellion, they are applied to for their aſſiſtance: But when they begin to enquire either into his politics, or his government, they are charged not to interfere: It is no buſineſs of theirs:—Such is the uſe of our conqueſts in India. By what machinery this ſtrange ſyſtem, apparently ſo contrary to reaſon, nature, common ſenſe, and common humanity, is ſet at work and ſupported, may be laid open to the public at ſome other time. The author of this little diſcuſſion has prepared a full, and as he thinks ſatisfactory explanation of it. Prudential reaſons

* What has been done to remedy this great abuſe within the laſt year, I am not acquainted; but thus things ſtood when the King of Tanjore was invaded.

induce

duce him to keep it back for the preſent; but it is not improbable that the activity of ſome perſons will compel him to produce it.

If we had conquered for ourſelves, if we had reſerved in the provinces, which have been ſubdued by our arms, any means of protection to the inhabitants; if we had put any ſort of check on the new deſpotiſm which we had ſet up, ſomething might be ſaid in favour of that ſeries of wars, which have brought ſuch deſtruction on our ſpecies. European oppreſſion has, in its worſt form, ſome traits of mildneſs in it; but we ſold both our virtues and vices to the Mahometans, and made the miſerable Indians pay the purchaſe.

It is not however enough, it ſeems, that many great and originally independent Indian Provinces, formerly kingdoms, have been ſubjected to the Mahometans. Tanjore alone (among many to whom the ſame juſtice is due) is reſcued, half ruined as it is; and this eſcape of an unhappy Prince and country, is repreſented to a Britiſh Parliament, and a Chriſtian people, as the greateſt of all ſubjects of ſorrow and lamentation.

One would really imagine, from the piteous complaints of the book before us, that the Nabob had been deprived of all his original territories; had been deſpoiled of all his private poſſeſſions; his women cruelly ſtripped of all the ornaments of their perſons; his houſe robbed to the bare walls; and his perſon mercileſsly impriſoned.—Theſe indeed are the

miſeries—

miseries—not which the Nabob has himself *suffered*, but those which he has *inflicted* on the King of Tanjore, and upon many other unredressed and helpless men, of great rank and distinction.—But when you hear him, or his advocates for him, talking to you of the * "good old Prince, "humbled into the dust before the servants of the Company;"—entreating Lord Pigot "to shew mercy to his "old age and white hairs;"—that "his dignity yielded to "his friendship;"—that "*a participation with his friends* was "his greatest pleasure;"—"to leave him in possession in *name* "*only*, to preserve his honour and character, and not to disgrace him in the eyes of Asia"—It is surely impossible for the hardest heart not to be touched—If after this pathetic peroration, you come to examine into the nature of the grievance which gives rise to so rueful a complaint, it will, I believe, excite some other passion rather than pity, when you find that the distress of the "good old Prince" is no more or less than this—That he has been helped by the English arms, to destroy not above twenty considerable Princes, a thousand times better men and better born than himself; that he has been enabled only to waste, rob, and oppress a vast tract of country, once the most populous and flourishing upon earth; that he has been able to engage us to make for him, no more than two cruel and unprovoked wars on the King of Tanjore; and in two years to rob him of no more than five millions of his money and effects. This is the subject of the complaint of "the good old prince;", this is what

* Considerations, P. 55 and 57.

has humbled him to the duſt; and it is for theſe indignities and injuries, that we are called upon to "have mercy on "his white hairs." It would provoke one's laughter, if it did not excite ſo much of our indignation, to ſee ſuch an audacious attempt made to pervert our benevolent natural feelings, and to debauch our ſympathy from the ſufferings of the oppreſſed, to beſtow them on the diſappointments of the oppreſſor; to divert our compaſſion from thoſe who complain, becauſe they endure great wrongs, to thoſe who raiſe an out-cry, becauſe they are not permitted to continue and increaſe them. It is hoped, however, that the active partizans of oppreſſion will do good at laſt; and, by officiouſly bringing thoſe matters into diſcuſſion, will rouze the humanity and juſtice of his Majeſty, this Nation, and the Company, in favour of the unhappy Nations, Princes, and People, who are under our protection, and from whom we derive infinite benefits.

APPENDIX.

Present establishment of the kingdom of Tanjore as settled by the Treaties of 1762 and 1769, by the order of the Court of Directors in 1775, and by the Conditions agreed on between the King and the East India Company in 1776; and which will scarcely be thought not sufficiently advantageous for the East India Company.

ARTICLES of Agreement between the King of Tanjore and the Nabob of Arcot *.

I. The King of Tanjore shall pay an annual Peshcuch or Tribute to the Mogul, of *two lacks of rupees*, and no more.

II. The King of Tanjore shall pay the further yearly sum of two lacks of rupees, and no more, in full for the usual and customary presents or Durbar charges †.

* Vid. Treaty and Agreement made and concluded between the Nabob of Arcot and the King of Tanjore in 1762. This treaty is guaranteed by the President and Council at Madrass, and approved by the Court of Directors.—Company's Appendix, P. 77 & seq.

† This and this only, is what the Nabob has any pretence to for his own profit; the treaty specifically distinguishes it from the Mogul's tribute.

III. The

III. The Nabob ſhall confirm to the King of Tanjore the full and free poſſeſſion of the diſtricts of Covilady and Elangad.

---

* In 1764 and 1765, diſputes ariſing concerning the banks of the river Cavery, the Preſidency of Madraſs are directed as guarantees of the treaty of 1762, to ſupport the King of Tanjore in his right to the repair of the ſaid banks; and the country of Tanjore muſt ſuffer famine, if the banks are not preſerved.

By the treaty with Hyder Ali in 1769, the peaceable poſſeſſion of his kingdom is ſecured and guaranteed to the Rajah of Tanjore.

* Vid. Comp. App. P. 86.

ARTICLES of Agreement between the King of Tanjore and the Eaſt India Company †.

I. The King of Tanjore ſhall admit a garriſon of the troops of the Company into the fort of Tanjore, and aſſign revenues ſufficient for the maintenance of the ſaid troops,

† Orders of the Court of Directors for the reſtoration of the King of Tanjore, and Lord Pigot's letter to the Court of Directors, 2d Sept. 1776.

and

and for providing military ſtores neceſſary for the defence of the garriſon *.

II. All repairs of fortifications ſhall be conducted by the Company's engineer at the King of Tanjore's expence; but no works or repairs ſhall be undertaken without his approbation and conſent, which ſhould always be ſignified in writing; nor until an eſtimate ſhall have been made of the charge to be incurred, and the meaſure fully approved and authoriſed by the Governor and Council.

III. No treaty with foreign powers ſhall be concluded by the King of Tanjore, without the Company's concurrence; nor ſhall any alliance be formed by him to their prejudice; nor any aid or aſſiſtance be given, directly or indirectly, to the enemies of the Britiſh nation.

IV. In caſe troubles ſhall ariſe in the kingdom of Tanjore, and the troops of the Company, or of the Nabob, ſhall march to the King of Tanjore's aſſiſtance at his requiſition, all extraordinary expences incurred thereby ſhall be defrayed by him, over and above the charges of the garriſon aforeſaid.

* The following are the inſtallments by which the King of Tanjore has ſtipulated to pay 400,000 pagodas annually, for the maintenance of troops.

In November	——	——	20,000
December	——	——	40,000
January	——	——	40,000
February	——	——	100,000
March	——	——	100,000
April (*a*)	——	——	100,000
			400,000

(*a*) Theſe ſix are the productive months.

V. No

V. No troops whatever, except those of the Company, shall be permitted to reside within the city of Tanjore, and except all such native * guards as may be necessary for supporting the dignity of his Majesty's government; and the number of such native guards shall be fixed by the Governor and Council, and not be exceeded or augmented by the King of Tanjore, on any account or pretence whatever.

VI. In regard to furnishing supplies in time of war, the King of Tanjore *shall not be obliged to comply with any requisition for troops, unless our Governor and Council join the Nabob in making such requisition*; nor shall the quota to be furnished to the Circar be left indefinite, but be limited to such supplies as shall on all occasions be deemed just and reasonable by the said Governor and Council; and the charge thereof, if defrayed by the King of Tanjore, shall be deducted from the annual tribute to be paid by him to the Nabob of the Carnatic.

VII. On the part of the Company it is stipulated, that no diminution of his authority over his subjects is intended by them; and that they will severely punish every military officer, or Company's servant, who shall in any respect interfere in the affairs of his government.

VIII. That particular accounts of the expence of the garrison shall be laid before him every three months, or so

* Tanjore Papers, vol i. p. 104. Rajah of Tanjore's letter to the governor. "For my body guard, I shall keep a body of men from one hundred to five hundred; and I want not to have one man, either horse or foot, more than that "number."

often as he ſhall require it; that no extravagance ſhall be permitted, nor any improper charge be allowed in ſuch accounts; and that if the annual amount thereof ſhall at any time be leſs than the revenues aſſigned to the Company, the ſurplus of the ſaid revenues ſhall be faithfully returned to him *; but if the expence of the garriſon ſhall exceed the amount of the revenues ſo aſſigned, then the King of Tanjore ſhall make good the deficiency.

IX. That if any diſputes ariſe reſpecting contingent or other expences, they ſhall be finally adjuſted by the King of Tanjore's agents, and our Preſident and Council, and not otherwiſe.

X. That the troops to be maintained by the King of Tanjore, ſhall be employed in his defence *alone*, ſo long as he keeps his faith with the Company.

XI. That no greater proportion of the revenues to be aſſigned to the Company, be required, than ſhall be deemed abſolutely neceſſary for the ſupport of the garriſon; but if any unforeſeen circumſtance ſhall render ſuch revenue inadequate thereto, the King of Tanjore muſt, as before obſerved, cauſe payment of the troops to be made from his other reſources.

* It is not the buſineſs at preſent, to enquire how far this and other parts of theſe ſtipulations have been obſerved by the Company's ſervants. It muſt not be doubted, that the Directors will, in their own time, effectually provide, that a country thus ſurrendered to their power will feel the benefit of their juſtice, and not be harraſſed by needleſs, unfounded, vexatious, and unjuſt demands.

F I N I S.